AMANDA COALIER
1479G N. Clybourn Ave, Chicago, Illinois 60610

D0515501

This edition published in 1993 by
SMITHMARK Publishers Inc.
16 East 32nd Street
New York, NY 10016

SMITHMARK books are available for bulk purchase
for sales promotion and premium use.
For details write or call the manager of special sales,
SMITHMARK Publishers Inc.
16 East 32nd Street
New York, NY 10016
212-532-6600

Produced by Wieser & Wieser, Inc.
118 East 25th Street
New York, NY 10010

Design: Tony Meisel

Printed in Spain by Cronion, S.A.

ISBN 0-8317-5167-3

Foreword

The cuisine of Mexico ranks among the greatest in the world–an opinion shared by a majority of the most discriminating gourmets. A Treasury of Mexican Cuisine is an homage to this great culinary tradition; however, this is intended to be something more than a mere cookbook: its words and pictures are meant to relate part of Mexico's history, with a sprinkling of anecdotes and legends that will show how this cuisine evolved.

    The recipes in this book have been carefully selected. There may be other versions of the same dishes, but much work, skill, knowledge, and, above all, experience, have gone into those included. We are confident that the special style and quality of the food presented in this book will dispel whatever erroneous beliefs about Mexican cuisine may be held in Mexico or elsewhere.

Contents

Introduction

Hernán Cortés and his followers came to the New World in search of gold, but they also found chocolate, peanuts, corn, tomatoes, squash, beans, avocados, vanilla, coconuts, chicle, tobacco and that noble and delectable bird, the turkey. The conquest of Mexico in 1521 gave rise to one of the richest culinary revolutions in history. For us today, it is impossible to conceive of the European and American diet before the sixteenth century: the Swiss without chocolate, the Italians without tomatoes, the Irish and Germans without potatoes and the American Thanksgiving without turkey.

At the same time, the native American cuisine became enriched by products introduced by the Spanish: beef, pork, lamb, citrus fruits, wheat, sugar, milk, cheese, garlic, vinegar and wine.

A third benefit, possibly the most important of all, came from the innumerable interactions of one cuisine with another. What many Mexicans assume to be native dishes, such as barbecued pig or Veracruz style red snapper, could not have existed before the Conquest. *Cochinita pibil* is a significant name, a combination of the Spanish word for "pig"–a Spanish import–and the Mayan word *pib,* meaning a pit in the ground where meat is cooked. Red snapper from the Gulf of Mexico prepared with native tomatoes and chiles would not have the same flavor were it not for the olives, garlic and limes of Spanish origin. This exchange of ingredients and cooking techniques is still going on. The cuisine of Mexico, like all other great cuisines, has always been open to outside influences.

Unlike the cuisine of Mexico's northern neighbors who adapted European cooking to suit New World ingredients, Mexican cuisine is not Spanish cooking adapted to American products, but is evolved directly from pre-Hispanic origins. Over the centuries, it has acquired a unique style and quality all its own.

Mexican cuisine dates from many centuries before the Conquest, and began in the reed huts of the pre-Hispanic inhabitants of America. The celebrated French gastronome, Auguste Escoffier wrote: "The history of the table of a nation is the reflection of its civilization. To show the changes in the order and serving of meals from century to century, to describe and comment on the progress. . .of [the] cuisine, is to paint a picture of the many stages through which a nation has evolved. . ."

There is no date on a calendar or dot on a map to mark the time and place of the beginning of what we know today as Mexican cuisine. It was a gradual process. The best way to explain what happened is to say that cooking became no longer exclusively Spanish and no longer exclusively Indian, and that the various combinations of the two produced the new and distinctive flavors and recipes that we now recognize as Mexican cuisine.

The new flavors of the Mexican cuisine emerged during the colonial period, principally in the bustling kitchens of the convents and monasteries and in the palaces of the wealthy. Tortillas were fried in the lard that the Spaniards had introduced, and lard was kneaded with *masa* (uncooked tortilla dough) to lighten it; milk replaced water in Moctezuma's favorite drink, hot chocolate, and sugar and vanilla were added; and fresh cheese adorned mounds of refried beans. That baroquely complicated sauce *mole poblano* was invented, and other new foods were created and given names.

The sugarcane cuttings planted shortly after Cortés landed thrived in the tropical lowlands of the conquered land, and produced sugar for a people whose only sweetening agents had been honey, *aguamiel* from the *maguey* cactus and a sticky yellow molasseslike substance from cornstalks. The new sweetener immediately appealed to the native palate. Not only was the flavor accepted with alacrity, but sugar served as an inspiration to the Mexican's artistic abilities, making "the confection of sweets, the most important Mexican craft," according to Florencio Gregori, the founder of the Mexican Academy of Gastronomy.

The making of candies and desserts, which had begun as a domestic undertaking, rapidly became an important national industry. Sugar was combined with almonds, apricots, figs, goat's milk, pumpkinseeds, liquors and peanuts, then sculpted into exotic shapes as diverse as snakes, flowers, cathedrals, skulls and fish.

The emerging Mexican cuisine was constantly being enriched by ingredients from other countries. Spain served New Spain as the conduit for new foods, recipes and ingredients from the Orient, Africa and other South American and Caribbean colonies. Examples of this are the secret of bread-making, which came from Egypt, passed through Spain, and ended up in America, and pasta, which traveled from ancient China to Italy and thence to Mexico. Beginning in 1571, a ship call the *Manila Galleon* made an annual voyage from the Phillipines to Acapulco, carrying rice, cloves, cinnamon, nutmeg, tea and other exotic products from the Orient.

Gastronomically speaking, the most important influences during the nineteenth century came from France. French influence had been felt in Mexico since long before Maximilian, for the political ideals generated by the French Revolution had greatly inspired the leaders of Mexican independence. All commercial ties with Spain were broken when Mexico won its independence, and a spirit of vindictiveness prevailed against the former oppressors. Mexico separated from Spain and grew closer to France.

The new aristocracy that developed during Díaz's rule was even more strongly imbued with the desire to imitate *la grande table* of France. Chefs, maîtres d's and gastronomes arrived in Mexico accompanied by crates of selected wines and exquisite culinary delicacies. Intricate French recipes gave Mexican cooking the elegant glaze that had characterized Escoffier's finest dishes. Many new shops, restaurants and specialty shops opened, and by the end of the nineteenth century, Mexico City had 80 bakeries, 1,500 grocery stores, 300 meat markets and 80 candy stores serving its population of 500,000.

For too many people, Mexican food means soggy, nondescript cornmeal objects topped with red-hot, greasy, suspicious-looking sauces. Another belief that is much too generally held is that a sine qua non of Mexican food is that it be blisteringly hot. Mexican food *is* usually heavily seasoned, but not necessarily hot, and any food, regardless of origin, will be too hot if there is too much chile in it, just as any food will be too salty if there is too much salt in it.

Good Mexican food ranges from mild, delicate fare such as light steamy tamales or duck covered with a subtle pumpkinseed sauce, to the spicy and hotter concoctions such as chile-laden Mexican green-tomato sauce. The degree of piquancy of every dish can be controlled by careful cooks who are the anonymous heroes and heroines of our story, be they famous chefs or nameless servants. Alexandre Dumas lamented the lack of glory awarded to those unsung heroes, saying that "a man who invents a new dish deserves more human gratitude than most emperors and generals." He believed that Careme was more deserving of status than Napoleon.

The discriminating traveler knows that when in Rome he or she must do as the Romans do. With few exceptions, the best Mexican food is found in Mexico, in the best restaurants and in hospitable city and country homes.

The purpose of this book is to provide recipes: some of the classic Mexican dishes, and to tell part of their stories. We hope that it will instruct, inform, delight and amuse the reader–making his or her mouth water all the while–and hopefully it will lead him or her to indulge the palate by cooking and eating true Mexican food.

Buen provecho y salud!

HOW TO USE THE RECIPES IN THIS BOOK
Unless otherwise indicated, all recipes yield six servings.

Many of the recipes require that ingredients be ground. In Mexican cooking it is always preferable to use the traditional stone mortar and pestle, called the *molcajete*. *Molcajetes* can be purchased in many gourmet food stores in the U.S. and Canada. A food processor can be used instead of a *molcajete,* but it should be used sparingly to keep the ingredients from turning into paste.

The preparation of chile will be a new technique for those not familiar with Mexican cooking. Specific instructions are given with each recipe containing chile.

There is a vocabulary in the back of the book to explain unfamiliar Mexican words.

Chicken Stock

Beef Stock

Basic Recipes

Chicken Stock

Yield: 16 cups of stock

1 broiler chicken, cut into pieces
1 head of garlic
2 large carrots, peeled and sliced
1 stalk celery
1 small leek
1 large onion
3 bay leaves
1 sprig fresh parsley
4 peppercorns
1 tablespoon salt
20 cups cold water

Wash the chicken and put it in a stew pot with the rest of the ingredients. Bring the mixture to a boil. Skim off the foam from the surface.

Cover the pot and cook over a low heat until the chicken is tender.

Let the broth cool. Skim off all excess grease. Remove the pieces of chicken. Strain.

Beef Stock

Yield: 16 cups of stock.

1 lb. chuck, cubed
1 lb. round
1 lb. beef ribs
1 knee or shank bone
1 head garlic
2 large carrots, peeled and sliced
1 stalk celery
1 small leek
1 large onion
3 bay leaves
1 sprig parsley
4 peppercorns
1 tablespoon salt
20 cups of cold water

Wash the meat and put in pot with water and the other ingredients. Bring to a boil. Let boil until foam appears on surface. Skim off foam.

Cover pot and simmer at low heat until meat is tender (about two hours).

Let cool and skim off fat. Remove and discard meat. Strain stock.

Fish Stock or Fumet

Yield: 16 cups of stock

1 fish head
1 leek
1 stalk celery
5 sprigs fresh coriander
1 onion
1 head garlic
3 bay leaves
1 tablespoon salt
20 cups water

Wash the fish and put it in a stew pot with the water and other ingredients. Let boil until foam appears on the surface. Skim off the foam.

Cover the pot and let simmer until the fish is tender.

Let the stock cool. Skim off all excess grease from the surface. Remove the fish, and strain.

Tortillas

Although millions of tortillas are sold daily in some parts of the United States, an enterprising cook may prefer homemade ones; and, since many of the recipes in this book call for fresh tortillas, we have included them in the list of basic recipes.

Masa is tortilla dough. It is usually available in parts of the United States with large Mexican-American populations. If *masa* is not available, Quaker makes a good corn flour for tortillas, which it markets as *masa harina*. Cornmeal is not suitable for tortilla making.

Yield: about 15 tortillas

1 1/4 cups, approximately, cold water
2 cups masa harina (see above)

Mix the water and flour to make a smooth dough. Let the dough stand for 20 minutes, then roll it into balls about 1 inch in diameter.

Line a small wicker basket or basket-shaped container with cotton napkins or cloths long enough to cover a stack of tortillas.

Fish Stock

Place each ball of dough between 2 sheets of polyethylene small enough to fit neatly into a tortilla press (available in gourmet shops). Close the press firmly, then open it again. Peel off one of the plastic sheets. If the dough sticks to the plastic, it is too moist, and more tortilla flour should be added. Gently lay the flattened dough round, uncovered side down, on a lightly greased, hot cast-iron griddle, skillet or *comal*. Peel off the remaining plastic sheet.

Cook one side for a short time, until the tortilla becomes a bit dry around the edges; then flip it over and cook for a bit longer on the second side. A tortilla should cook in about 2 minutes; a skilled cook can make more than one at a time.

As each tortilla is cooked, put it in the napkin-lined basket and wrap the excess folds of napkin around it to keep it warm. Continue this procedure until the tortillas form a neat stack.

Frozen and canned tortillas are also available in the United States and can be used instead of homemade ones, but such tortillas will have already been cooked, and should merely be heated in a steamer or a microwave oven.

Antojitos

CORN: THE BASIS OF MEXICAN CIVILIZATION

Mexico is the birthplace of corn. The first identifiable plants have been traced to the valleys of Mexico and Tehuacan. Prehistoric nomads ate the wild seeds of the *teozintle* ("divine corn" in Nahuatl), and after centuries of selection and crossbreeding, developed the corn we know today. Without the presence of corn, Cortés probably would have found only wandering tribes of hunters.

Many different varieties of corn are found in Mexico. Some ears are short and stubby, others long and slim. Kernels vary in shape and texture, from succulent and plump to small and hard. Their colors range from blue-green to pale creamy yellow.

And the variety of corn is nothing compared to its uses in Mexican cuisine. An ear of corn may be boiled or broiled, garnished with powdered chili and grated cheese and eaten off the cob. Mature, dried ears are harvested and the kernels made into the dough called *masa,* the base for tortillas, tamales and *atoles.*

The tortilla is the single most important element in Mexican cuisine. Author Diana Kennedy says that the tortilla "is perhaps the most versatile piece of foodstuff the world has known." It replaces bread as the accompaniment to Mexican meals. Wrap something in a tortilla–roasted pork, chicken, refried beans, squash flowers–and it becomes a *taco,* the most popular dish in the country. Stuff a tortilla, wrap it tight, fix it with a toothpick and lightly fry it, and it becomes a *bocadillo* (nibble) or an *antojito* (appetizer) to accompany beverages or tease the palate before a meal.

"Frugal Mexican cooks use hardened leftover tortillas to make *totopos, gordas,* and *bolitas.* They turn up in soups, in casseroles and as tasty snacks. The Mayans had an early form of enchilada called *papadzules* of "food for the lords."

Besides tortillas, *masa* can be made into *quesadillas, garnachas* and *chalupas,* little "boats" to be filled with shredded chicken and bathed in sauce.

Tamales, too, in infinite variety, stem from corn. So does *pozole,* the hearty soup from the state of Jalisco.

The cuisine of Mexico is ample testimony that corn ranks with wheat and rice as one of the great staples of the world, and is arguably, the most versatile of all.

Sopes

(small garnished fried tortillas)

2 cups masa harina
1 1/3 cups water
Salt to taste
1 cup oil
1 cup refried beans (see index)
Meat from 2 chicken legs and 2 thighs, shredded
6 lettuce leaves, finely chopped
1/4 onion, chopped
1 cup cream
1 cup sauce of your choice (see index "Sauces and Chiles")

Mix the *masa,* water and salt to form a dough. Make little balls of dough of the right size to form tortillas that will be about 2 1/2 inches in diameter when flattened in the tortilla press. After flattening, let them stand for 24 hours.

Just before serving, fry the tortillas in the oil. Drain.

Spread refried beans on top of the tortillas. Sprinkle with the shredded chicken, lettuce and onion. Top each with a tablespoon of cream and the sauce you have chosen. Serve immediately.

Chilaquiles

(casserole of tortilla strips, chicken and green sauce)

12 tortillas (see index), one day old
1/2 cup oil
2 cups green sauce (see index)
1 cup chicken stock (see index)
1 sprig epazote
Salt to taste
1 onion, sliced into rings, and blanched in cold water
2 cups mild white cheese, crumbled

Cut the tortillas into 1 1/2 inch squares. Let them dry on a flat surface in a warm place. Then fry in hot oil until they are brown and crisp. Remove from pan and drain.

Heat the sauce with the stock and *epazote*. Bring to a boil, and add salt. Remove from the stove and keep in a warm place.

Let the tortillas stand in the sauce for five minutes before serving. Serve on warm plates, garnished with onion rings and crumbled cheese .

Note: Hot shredded chicken is often sprinkled on top of the chilaquiles.

Enchiladas de Mole

(tortillas filled with chicken in *mole* sauce)

18 tortillas (see index)
1/4 cup oil
1 tablespoon oil
1/8 small onion, finely chopped
*Meat from 2 chicken thighs and 2 legs, cooked
and shredded*
1/4 cup mole poblano sauce (see index)
3 cups mole poblano
3 tablespoons toasted sesame seeds
1 onion, sliced into rings and blanched
1 cup mild white cheese, crumbled

Fry the tortillas lightly in oil. Remove before they
become crisp.

In a separate pan, fry the onion lightly in hot
oil. Add the shredded chicken and mix well. Add
1/4 cup of *mole* and stir until the chicken is totally
coated with the sauce.

Bring 3 cups of *mole* to a boil, and then
remove it from the heat. Dip the tortillas one by
one into the *mole*. Then put several strips of
shredded chicken on each tortilla, roll the tortilla
up, place it on a serving dish and cover it with
mole.

Sprinkle 1/2 tablespoon of sesame seeds, a few
onion rings and some crumbled cheese over each
serving, and serve immediately.

13

Tacos

(rolled tortillas with various meat fillings)

Tacos can have an infinite variety of fillings. Here we give the recipes for three.

POTATO AND *CHORIZO*
(PORK SAUSAGE) TACOS
(yields 6 tacos)

1/2 cup pork sausage, crumbled
1 cup cooked potatoes, cut into small cubes
1/8 onion, finely chopped
6 hot tortillas

Cook the sausage in a hot skillet. When it begins to give off fat, add the potatoes and onion. Fry the mixture well. Put a tablespoon of the sausage mixture on each tortilla, and fold into a taco. Serve immediately.

CHICKEN AND *MOLE* TACOS
(yields 6 tacos)

1 cup mole sauce (see index)
6 tablespoons chicken, cooked and shredded
6 hot tortillas

Heat the *mole*. Add the chicken and cook the mixture until it boils. Put one tablespoon of the

mixture on each tortilla. Fold to form a taco. Serve immediately.

CARNITAS (PORK TACOS)
(yields 6 tacos)

1 pound carnitas *(see index)*
6 hot tortillas

Cut the pork into small chunks and heat in a frying pan. Put a tablespoonful of pork on each tortilla. Roll up to form a taco.

Note: Tacos can be served with *guacamole* (see index) or with any of the sauces mentioned in this book.

Quesadillas
(fried tortillas with cheese filling)

2 cups masa harina
Water
Salt to taste
2 ounces asadero *cheese, or any good melting cheese, cut into pencil-thin strips*
2 sprigs epazote
1 cup oil

Follow the procedure for making tortillas (see index). Make round balls big enough to produce tortillas 4 inches in diameter when flattened.

Put two strips of cheese and a few *epazote* leaves in the center of each uncooked tortilla. Fold the tortilla in half.

Fry the folded dough in hot oil until it browns. Drain on absorbent paper.

Serve the *quesadillas* immediately. Accompany with guacamole (see index) and/or any of the sauces mentioned in this book.

Note: Quesadillas can also be made with squash blossoms, mushrooms, mashed potatoes and/or *huitlacoche* fillings.

Tostadas de Jalisco

(toasted tortillas topped with chicken and other ingredients)

12 *one day old tortillas*
l/2 cup oil or lard
1 cup refried beans (see index)
Meat from three pieces of chicken, cooked and shredded
1/2 head lettuce, finely chopped
1 cup heavy cream or sour cream
6 chiles chipotles *in vinegar, seeded and finely chopped*

1/2 onion, sliced into rings
2 avocados, cut into strips
1 cup mild white cheese, crumbled
6 radishes, cut into thin rounds

Spread a thin coating of oil or lard over the tortillas. Put them in a warm oven until they are crisp. Remove from the oven and let cool. Spread a layer of refried beans on top of each tortilla, then sprinkle with chicken, lettuce and cream, and garnish with bits of chile, onion, avocado, cheese and radishes.

More chile *chipotle* can be served as a side dish, if desired.

AVOCADOS: AN AZTEC APHRODISIAC

The word *avocado* is a combination of two Nahuatl words: *ahuacatl,* meaning "testicle," and *cuahuitl,* meaning "tree." The avocado tree is believed to have been sacred to the Aztecs, and its fruit was considered an aphrodisiac by both pre- and post-Hispanic people. The sixteenth century botanist Francisco Hernández described the tree as being "similar to an oak tree," with a fruit that "excites extraordinarily the venerous appetites." He added, "This remarkable fruit is also nutritious." Other early botanists recommended avocados as a cure for dysentery and a way to prevent baldness.

Avocados, also called *alligator pears,* vary in size, shape, color and flavor, but the type most prized in Mexico is the small variety with a thin, nearly black skin with a very slight flavor of anise. Avocado leaves, dried or fresh, are used to accent certain dishes, as they give off the same nutty flavor as the fruit. In northern Mexico, a dash of grated avocado pit is used to flavor a sauce used in enchiladas.

The avocado is an indigenous Mexican fruit, but it adapted and thrived immediately when introduced elsewhere, particularly along the shores of the Mediterranean, and later in the Pacific Islands, especially in the Philippines. The young George Washington is believed to have eaten an avocado in 1751 during a trip to Barbados; but it was not until 1831 that Mexican avocados were planted in the United States, first in Florida and then, in 1871, in California.

Avocados are a versatile fruit. They are sublime when eaten with just a pinch of salt or a few drops of lime juice. They are tasty when cut into thick slices, or used as garnish for *tostadas,* in a shrimp or abalone cocktail, or cut in half and filled with vinaigrette sauce or small eels. Avocados make excellent soup and they can be pureed and sweetened to make ice cream or mousse. Perhaps the best-known way to prepare avocados is as *guacamole.* The word *guacamole* is derived from *ahuacatl* and *molli,* a "mixture" or "concoction."

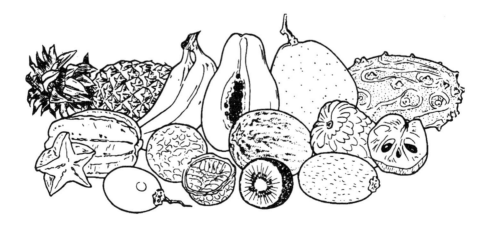

Sopa de Lima

(soup made from a unique Yucatecan lime)

6 tortillas, one day old
1/8 cup oil
1/6 cup oil
1 medium onion, finely chopped
1 clove garlic, finely chopped
1 large green pepper, finely chopped
2 large tomatoes, peeled, seeded and finely chopped
3 limas*
6 cups chicken stock (see index)
Meat from 1 large chicken breast, poached and shredded
1 lime

Use scissors to cut the tortillas into long, pencil-thin strips. Put them on a flat pan and let them dry for about 30 minutes in a warm place. When they are dry, fry them in 1/8 cup of oil until they are crisp and golden brown. Drain.

Heat 1/6 cup of oil in a skillet, and lightly fry the onion, garlic and green pepper. Add the chopped tomatoes and stir constantly until the mixture forms a paste.

Peel the *limas* and separate into sections. Remove the outer membranes and seeds. Squeeze the juice from the fruit (if the *limas* are not cleaned thoroughly, the juice will have a bitter taste).

Heat the broth, and add the shredded chicken. Then combine it with the tomato mixture. Add the strained *lima* juice.

Cut the lime into thin round slices. Line the bottoms of heated bowls with the tortilla strips, and then put slices of the lime on top of the strips. Pour the hot soup into the bowls. Serve immediately.

If Yucatecan limas are not available, ordinary limes may be used instead, adding at the same time one teaspoon of lime concentrate.

18

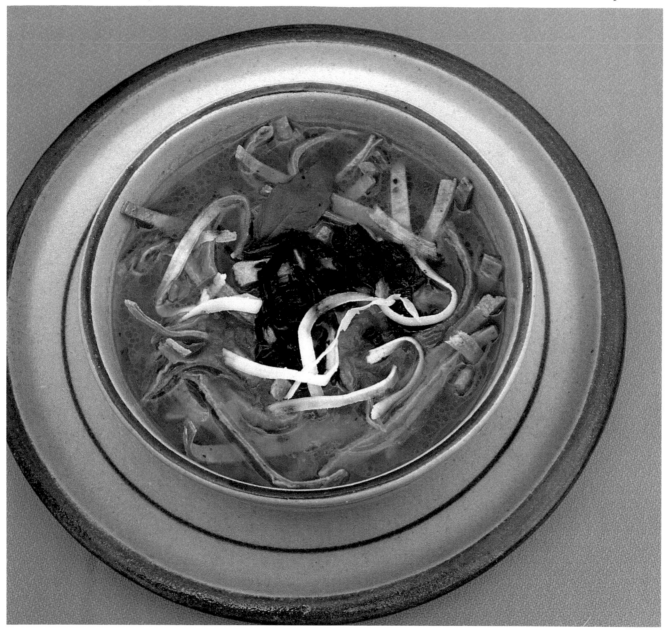

Sopa de Tortilla

(tortilla soup)

12 one day old tortillas
1/4 cup oil
1/8 cup oil
1/4 medium onion, finely chopped
2 cloves garlic, finely chopped
4 tomatoes, skinned, seeded and ground
6 cups chicken stock (see index)
2 sprigs epazote
Salt to taste
10 ounces mild white cheese, crumbled
6 chiles pasilla, *fried and chopped*

Use scissors to cut the tortillas into pencil-thin strips. Put them on a flat surface and let them dry for about 30 minutes in a warm place. Then fry them in 1/4 cup of oil until they are brown. Drain.

Lightly fry the onion and garlic in 1/8 cup of oil. Add the tomatoes, and stir constantly until the ingredients form a thick paste. Add the stock and *epazote*. Cover and let simmer over a low heat. Add salt. Strain, but keep the liquid hot.

Line the bottoms of hot soup bowls with the tortilla strips. Then pour the soup into the bowls or mugs and sprinkle cheese and chopped chile on the soup. Serve immediately.

19

Caldo de Habas

(dried fava-bean soup)

5 cups dried, peeled fava beans
2 quarts water
1 chile pasilla, *cleaned, with the veins removed,*
and fried in oil
1/4 cup oil
1/2 large onion, finely chopped
2 cloves garlic, finely chopped
4 tomatoes, peeled, seeded and finely chopped
3 sprigs fresh coriander, finely chopped
3 sprigs fresh mint, finely chopped
1 sprig epazote
3 bay leaves
Salt to taste
4 chiles pasilla, *cleaned with the veins removed,*
chopped, and fried in olive oil

Soak the fava beans in water for 3 hours. Then simmer for 1 1/2 hours. When they are soft, add one chile *pasilla*.

Fry the onion and garlic lightly in hot oil. Add the chopped tomatoes and salt. Stir constantly until the mixture forms a smooth paste. Add the paste to the bean mixture, along with the coriander, mint, *epazote* and bay leaves. Simmer the soup until the beans have begun to disintegrate. Add salt to taste. Serve in hot soup bowls.

Put the olive oil and chopped chiles in separate serving dishes on the table, so that each person can help him or herself.

Caldo Michi

(a light fish soup)

1/4 cup oil
2 medium onions, finely chopped
4 cloves garlic, chopped
2 bay leaves
5 tomatoes, peeled, seeded and chopped
1 sprig fresh oregano
3 chiles jalapeños, seeded and chopped
1 white-meat fish (approximately 4 pounds), cut into thick steaks*
6 cups fumet (see index)
2 sprigs parsley
Salt to taste
2 sprigs fresh coriander, finely chopped
Lemon wedges

Lightly fry the onions and bay leaves in hot oil. Add the tomatoes. Stir constantly until the mixture forms a paste. Add the oregano, chile and fish. Mix well. Add the fumet, and stir constantly but carefully so that the fish does not disintegrate. Add parsley and salt.

Simmer the soup over a low heat until it boils. Remove the parsley. Put a fish steak at the bottom of each soup bowl, and pour the hot liquid over the fish. Sprinkle with chopped coriander and garnish with lemon wedges before serving.

* Red snapper, snook or any other good-quality fish with white meat will do.

Sopa de Elote con Rajas a la Poblana

(corn soup with strips of chile, Puebla style)

2 chiles poblanos
1/4 cup oil
1/4 medium onion, ground
3 cloves garlic, ground
1 large tomato, peeled, seeded and ground
6 cups chicken stock (see index)
Kernels from 2 fresh ears of corn
Salt to taste
10 ounces of mild white cheese, cut into strips
about 4 x 2 x 1/2 inches

Toast the chiles over a flame or under a broiler until the skin blisters and chars slightly. Wrap them in a cloth or a plastic bag for about 30 minutes until they "sweat" and the skin loosens. Remove the skins and veins. Cut the chiles into long narrow strips.

Fry the onion and garlic lightly in hot oil. Add the tomato and stir until the mixture forms a smooth paste. Add the stock. When the soup comes to a boil, skim off the grease. Add the corn kernels, and let the soup simmer until the kernels are tender. Add the chiles, and continue boiling until they are soft.

Serve the soup in hot soup bowls or mugs. Garnish with cheese, and serve immediately.

TOMATOES: THE LOVE APPLE

It took centuries for the tomato, a native Mexican plant, to outlive a very bad reputation and gain acceptance in European and North American cuisines, and then become a basic ingredient in cooking the world over. Although cultivated and eaten in Mexico and Peru long before the Conquest, the first plants grown in Europe were considered a mere botanical curiosity whose fruit was definitely not to be eaten, since it was a member of the poisonous nightshade family. In the middle of the eighteenth century, brave Spanish monks dared to eat the suspicious fruit, and recorded it as an ingredient in their recipes. Later, the French began to cultivate tomatoes, considering its fruit to be a powerful aphrodisiac. For this reason, they called tomatoes *pommes d'amour.*

Many English-speaking people are surprised to learn that a word in their language comes from the Nahuatl, the language of the Aztecs. The word *tomato* comes from *tomatl* in Nahuatl, and in Spanish carries the prefix *ji,* meaning "red." The Spanish made the distinction between *jitomate* and *tomate* because they were naming two different fruits.

Having overcome this bad reputation, the tomato now ranks third among vegetable crops in the United States. (Technically, a tomato is a fruit, but it is commonly considered a vegetable because of how it is used.)

The *tomate,* or Mexican green tomato, is a basic ingredient in Mexican cuisine. It is not an unripe tomato, but another fruit altogether. A relative of the Cape gooseberry, Mexican green tomatoes, or *tomatillos,* are about the size of a small plum and have a parchmentlike husk on the outside.

Red tomatoes are a familiar ingredient in most cuisines and are used in so many different ways, from pasta sauces to soups, stews, marmalades and salads, that they need little introduction. But the Mexican green tomato is unique to Mexican cooking and lends flavor and color to many sauces, among them Mexican green sauce and *salsa cascabel.*

Huevos en Rabo de Mestiza

(eggs poached in a chile and tomato broth)

3 chiles poblanos
1/3 cup oil
1/2 large onion, finely chopped
2 cloves garlic, finely chopped
1 bay leaf
1/8 teaspoon powdered thyme
6 medium tomatoes, peeled, seeded and ground
1 1/2 cups chicken stock (see index)
Salt to taste
12 eggs
6 slices of a soft, mild white cheese, crumbled

Toast the chiles directly over an open flame or under the broiler, until the skin blisters and chars slightly. Wrap them in a cloth or plastic bag until they "sweat" and the skin loosens. Split them open and remove the skins, veins and seeds. Wash the chiles and cut them into long narrow strips.

Fry the onion, garlic, bay leaf and thyme lightly in hot oil. Then add the tomatoes, stirring constantly until the mixture forms a thick paste. Add the chicken stock and salt, and cook over a low heat until the mixture comes to a boil.

Strain the mixture, and bring it to a boil again. Drop the raw eggs into the hot sauce, one by one, until they are poached. Add the cheese and the chile strips. Cook for 4 minutes more.

To serve, put the eggs on the bottom of a serving dish, then place the chile strips over the eggs and cover with the tomato sauce.

Huevos Motuleños

(eggs in a sauce from Motul, Yucatán)

6 tortillas
1/4 cup oil
1 cup refried beans (see index), pureed
1/4 onion
2 cloves garlic
2 tomatoes
4 chiles serranos
1/4 cup beef stock (see index)
Salt to taste
1 tablespoon oil
1/2 cup cooked peas
2 slices ham, diced
1/2 cup oil
12 eggs
2 plantains, sliced lengthwise into strips and fried
1 cup añejo or Romano cheese, grated

Fry the tortillas in 1/4 cup of oil and drain. Spread refried beans over one side of each tortilla. Keep warm.

Toast the onion, garlic, tomato and chiles on a hot griddle or *comal,* until they are slightly charred. Peel the tomatoes. Grind the toasted ingredients and mix them with the beef stock. Season with salt. Heat 1 tablespoon of oil in a skillet. Add the mixture, and fry. Then add the peas and the ham.

In a separate pan, fry the eggs in 1/2 cup of oil. Put two fried eggs on top of each tortilla, and cover with the sauce.

Garnish with plantains and grated cheese. Serve immediately.

Huevos Rancheros

(fried eggs with ranchero sauce)

1/4 cup oil
6 tortillas
12 eggs
l/2 cup oil
Salsa ranchera *(see index)*

Fry the tortillas lightly in 1/4 cup of oil, and remove while still soft. Put a tortilla on each plate.

Fry the eggs in oil two at a time. Put two eggs on top of each tortilla .

Cover the eggs with *salsa ranchera,* and serve immediately.

Machaca Norteña

(scrambled eggs with shredded beef jerky)

1/4 cup oil
1/2 medium onion, finely chopped
3 chiles serranos, *chopped*
9 tablespoons beef jerky, dried and shredded
12 eggs, beaten
Wheat-flour tortillas

Lightly fry the onion and chiles in hot oil. Add the meat and continue frying. Add the eggs, stirring constantly. When the eggs are cooked, remove from heat and serve immediately, with hot wheat-flour tortillas.

Fish & Seafood

BEER AND WINE:
AMIGOS OF MEXICAN CUISINE

"Beer is the perfect accompaniment to a Mexican meal . . . and Mexican beers can hold their own against, and more often than not surpass, those brewed in other parts of the world. A well-chilled stein of draught beer and a plate of *ceviche* make an unbeatable combination," according to Diana Kennedy, leading authority on Mexican cuisine. One good reason is that a cold glass of beer is a refreshing draught with highly seasoned Mexican food, but the best reason is simply that it tastes good. Like vodka and caviar, milk and cookies, or cheese and wine, it is a perfect marriage.

Since the Spaniards were slow to acquire a taste for native beverages like *pulque,* made from the *maguey* cactus, they introduced wine and beer to the New World to quench their thirst. Only a few years after the Conquest, barley and grapes were under cultivation, and by 1542, King Charles of Spain granted Alfonso de Herrera, one of Cortés' officers, a license to produce beer in New Spain, thus establishing the first Mexican brewery. Beer was made initially from a mixture of barley, sugar, lemon and tamarind, a recipe that seems to have been successful. Herrera boasted to the king that locally produced beer "was becoming a favorite drink of the Viceroy, the Spaniards and certain natives of the land, who prefer it to their *pulque.*" Later, the skills and knowledge of several German and Swiss brewers permitted Mexican beer production to attain industrial proportions.

Today, seventeen breweries produce a great variety of excellent beers, ranging from a light Pilsner type to a medium or Viennese beer to a dark, heavy Munich brew, all marketed under different brand names, and many of which are sold in the United States and other countries. Barley is grown in the central highlands in the states of Hidalgo, Puebla and Mexico. Although Mexico has a great variety of climates, none is suited to growing hops, so brewers must import this indispensable ingredient from the United States.

Mexicans drink quantities of beer–some thirty-nine liters per capita annually, compared with a half-liter of wine. Though a less popular beverage, Mexican wines are coming into their own after centuries of fighting for survival against wines from Spain.

In 1523, three years after Cortés uncorked the first bottle of wine in the New World to celebrate his victory in Tenochtitlán, he ordered the planting of the first vineyards in America, which consisted of five thousand vines for every hundred Indians living on each estate. But in the mid-sixteenth century, Philip II banned the cultivation of grapes in the New World to protect the lucrative Spanish wine-exporting business.

Today, five large distilleries produce over a million cases of wine annually, and although the quality varies greatly from bottle to bottle, very good Pinot Noirs, Chenin Blancs, Cabernet Sauvignons and Colombards are available. Mexican vintners seem determined to be the exception to the rule that "a country that produces good beer makes bad wine, and vice versa."

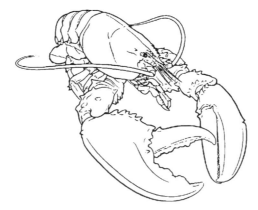

Huachinango a la Veracruzana

(red snapper, Veracruz style)

6 fillets red snapper
Salt and white pepper to taste
Juice of 3 limes
1 cup flour
1 cup oil
3 cloves garlic
1/2 large onion, cut into rings
3 pimientos, seeded and cut in long strips
3 bay leaves
1/2 teaspoon powdered thyme
6 tomatoes, toasted, peeled, seeded and ground
4 cups fish stock (see index)
Salt to taste
1/2 cup green olives
6 chiles chilacas *in vinegar*
Tortillas

Wash the fillets and season them with salt and pepper. Place them on a flat plate and sprinkle them with lime juice. Let stand for 10 minutes, then pat dry with a paper towel. Dredge both sides lightly in flour. In a skillet, fry the fillets on both sides in hot oil. (Remove when they become light brown.) Drain, retaining oil.

In the same oil, fry the garlic until it browns, then remove it, and fry the onion, pimientos, bay leaves and thyme. Add tomatoes, stirring until the mixture is well blended. Add the hot stock, season with salt, and bring to a boil.

Then add the olives, the fillets and the chiles *chilacas* and simmer over a low heat for 10 minutes, or until the chile flavor has penetrated the sauce.

Serve in deep soup bowls. Accompany with hot tortillas.

Ceviche Acapulqueño

(raw fish marinated in lime juice)

2 pounds Spanish or king mackerel, filleted*
Juice of 20 limes
Salt to taste
5 tomatoes, peeled, seeded and chopped
1 large onion, finely chopped
3 chiles serranos, finely chopped
7 sprigs fresh coriander, finely chopped
1/8 cup olive oil
White pepper to taste
1 avocado, cut into strips

Wash the fish fillets, remove the skin and dark meat, and dice into 3/4-inch cubes.

Put the diced fish in a glass, porcelain, earthenware, plastic or stainless-steel bowl (never in a wooden or non-stainless-steel bowl or in a bowl of any other metal). Cover completely with the lime juice. Season with salt. Let the fish marinate for about three hours, stirring occasionally with a wooden, ceramic or plastic spoon. Make sure that the fish is always covered with lime juice.

When the fish has attained an even, perfectly paper-white color, add the tomatoes, onion, chile, coriander, oil and pepper, and mix thoroughly. Keep in refrigerator until ready to serve.

Garnish with avocado strips before serving.

* Red snapper or snook can be substituted for mackerel.

28

Rebanadas de Mero en Escabeche

(soused or pickled fish)

6 fresh grouper steaks about 1 inch thick*
4 cloves garlic
3 cloves
6 teaspoons black peppercorns
5 oregano leaves
1 tablespoon achiote *paste*
Juice of 1 large Seville orange
Salt to taste
1/8 cup olive oil
6 cloves garlic
1 large onion, sliced into rings
2 tomatoes, skinned, peeled and cut into rounds
1 pimiento, cut into strips
1/2 cup fresh parsley, finely chopped
1 cup fish stock (see index), or water
7/8 cup olive oil

Wash the fish and pat dry with paper towels.

Grind together 4 cloves of garlic, cloves, peppercorns and oregano. Add the *achiote* and the orange juice. Stir until the mixture becomes a smooth paste. Add salt. Cover the fish on both sides with the paste, and let stand for 1 hour.

Fry 6 cloves of garlic in l/8 cup of olive oil over a high heat. Remove the garlic, fry the onion in the oil, and then remove the onion.

In the same pan, sprinkle the fillets with a little olive oil, then fry them on both sides in some more olive oil. Cover the fried fillets with the onion rings, pimientos and parsley, add the stock and the remaining oil, and let simmer over a low heat until the liquid has been absorbed.

* Red snapper or snook can be substituted for grouper.

29

Huachinango a la Talla

(barbecued red snapper)

1 large red snapper, about 3 pounds
Juice of 4 limes
Salt to taste
2 tomatoes, peeled and seeded
1 medium onion
3 cloves garlic
3 teaspoons achiote
Juice of 4 oranges
2 tablespoons vinegar
2 bay leaves
1 sprig thyme
1 sprig fresh coriander

Clean the fish, and butterfly it. Remove the bones. Sprinkle the lime juice and salt over both sides of the fish. Let stand for 15 minutes.

Grind together the tomatoes, onion, garlic, *achiote*, orange juice, vinegar, bay leaves; thyme and coriander, forming a paste. Add salt to taste. Cover both sides of the fish with the paste, and let stand for 2 hours.

Put the fish in a baking dish, and cover with aluminum foil. Cook in a medium oven (about 350 degrees) until the fish is done (approximately 45 minutes).

Place the fish in a hot serving dish, and pour the sauce over.

Jaibas Rellenas a la Tampiquena
(stuffed crabs, tampico style)

1/4 cup oil
1/2 small onion, finely chopped
1/2 clove garlic, finely chopped
2 tomatoes, peeled, seeded and ground
Meat from 15 large crabs (about 1 1/2 pounds)
1/2 cup green olives, chopped
1/4 cup capers, chopped
3 chiles serranos, seeds and veins removed
Salt and pepper to taste
6 clean crab shells
6 teaspoons bread crumbs

Heat the oil in a pan. Fry the onion and the garlic lightly. Add the tomatoes, stirring constantly until a paste is formed. Add the crab, olives, capers and chiles. Season with salt and pepper, and stir the mixture until blended.

Fill the shells with the crab mixture, and sprinkle with bread crumbs. Brown under a broiler, and serve immediately.

Camarones a la Mexicana

(shrimp, Mexican style)

2 pounds large, uncooked shrimp, shelled and
cleaned
Juice of 3 large limes
Salt and pepper to taste
5 chiles anchos, seeds and veins removed
1 cup vinegar
1 tablespoon powdered oregano
2 cups olive oil
6 cloves garlic
2 large onions
2 bay leaves
2 cups hot water
6 chiles jalapeños in vinegar
1 onion, sliced into rings.

Cover the shrimp with lime juice, season with salt
and pepper and let stand for 1 hour.

Soak the chiles *anchos* in the vinegar until they
become soft.

Mix the oregano with the olive oil, then heat
the oil, and fry the shrimp in it. Remove the
shrimp when they are cooked. Drain, saving the
oil.

Grind the chiles with the vinegar, garlic and
onion. Then fry in the same oil used to fry the
shrimp. Add the shrimp, bay leaves and hot water.
Cook until the sauce thickens.

Serve on hot plates. Garnish with chiles
jalapeños and onion rings.

Main Dishes

MOLE POBLANO:
MEXICO'S PIECE DE RESISTANCE

Whenever there is an occasion for celebration in Mexico–a wedding, a birthday, the blessing of a new house or new tractor, a graduation, All Saint's Day–*mole is* served. *Mole poblano* is fiesta food, the nation's *pièce de résistance,* the touchstone of its cuisine. To refuse a plate of *mole* borders on treason.

Mole, a thick, heavy, dark brown sauce is an uncanny combination of native ingredients–chile, chocolate (humorists have called *mole* "hot-fudge chicken") tomatoes and tortillas–mixed with ingredients from the Old World–almonds, raisins, garlic and bread–and flavored with Oriental spices–cinnamon and cloves. Many hours of hard work plus some culinary skill are needed to prepare a good *mole.*

Entire books have been written about *mole;* songs have been composed about it and children chant *"Mole sin ajonjolí, ni para mí ni para tí"* ("Mole without ajonjolí (sesame seeds), neither for you nor for me"). And adults who have eaten an excess of *mole* grouse, *"Pa' qué quiero más agruras, si con mole ya me basta,"* which loosely translates "More heartburn I do not desire, as my *mole* keeps me on fire."

The word *mole* has transcended gastronomic significance and acquired meaning as a synonym for "the ideal, the best." To say to someone that he is your *mero mole* is to say that he is the best, the tops; or to be in one's *mero mole* is to be extremely happy.

Although there are many versions of the origins of *mole poblano,* the most popular is that it was born in the seventeenth century in the Convent of Santa Clara (the only birth ever recorded there), in the city of Puebla de los Angeles. The legend is that in the convent a banquet was to be held. For the event, Mother Superior Andrea exerted her culinary imagination and produced the first *mole poblano.* Another version of the origin of *mole* has a friar named Fray Pascual going into the monastery kitchen to supervise a meal. Angered by the disorder he found, Fray Pascual gathered all the ingredients

scattered about the messy kitchen, and threw them into a large earthenware pot in which a turkey was stewing. The result of this fortuitous combination of ingredients was *mole poblano.*

The nuns from the Convent of Santa Monica in Puebla believe that an authentic *mole poblano* must contain coriander and a piece of pork; those from the Convent of Santa Teresa use different quantities and kinds of chiles. For some cooks, onions are a must, while for others they are taboo; still others believe that the turkey will not have the correct flavor unless chile *chipotle* has been added while it stews.

Two other kinds of *mole* deserve mention: *mole de olla* and *mole verde. Mole de olla* (literally, "*mole* from an earthenware pot") is a simple, hearty soup made from pork and beef, which are boiled until tender and combined with zucchini squash, string beans, chiles, corn on the cob, garlic, potatoes, *chayote* and *epazote. Mole verde* (literally, "green *mole*") is a thick, pale green sauce prepared from ground pumpkinseeds, green tomatoes, lettuce leaves and herbs, in which meat or fowl is cooked. It is delicate, mild and delicious.

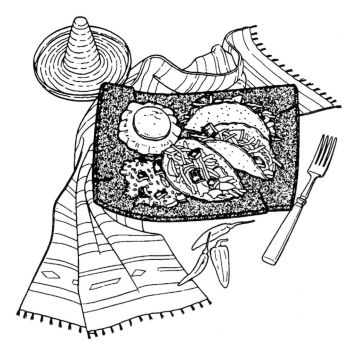

Mole Poblano

(Mole, Puebla style)

6 pieces boiled chicken
6 cups chicken stock (see index)
6 chiles mulatos
4 chiles anchos
2 chiles pasilla
2 tablespoons lard
2 tablespoons toasted sesame seeds
3 heaping tablespoons almonds
2 tablespoons peanuts, shelled and peeled
2 tablespoons raisins
1/2 hard roll
1 tortilla
1/8 teaspoon anise seeds
3 whole cloves
1 medium tomato, peeled and seeded
1/4 medium onion
2 cloves garlic
2 tablespoons lard
2 ounces chocolate
1 tablespoon sugar
2 small cinnamon sticks
2 teaspoons of salt
3 heaping tablespoons toasted sesame seeds

Clean the chicken, cut it into pieces and boil it in the stock until tender.

Wash the chiles. Cut them open and remove veins and seeds. Fry them in hot lard, drain, and soak for 15 minutes in two cups of the chicken stock. Then grind the chiles with this broth to form a paste.

In the lard used to fry the chiles, fry the sesame seeds, almonds, peanuts, raisins, bread, tortilla, anise, cloves, tomato, onion and garlic. Grind all ingredients together with the lard and two more cups of the chicken broth. Strain the mixture, and then grind it again until it becomes a smooth paste.

Heat another portion of lard in a large earthenware pot, and fry the almond and bread mixture in it, stirring constantly, until the grease floats to the surface. Add the strained chile mixture, stirring constantly until the grease again floats to the surface. Add the chocolate, cinnamon, sugar and salt. If the sauce is too thick, add more broth. Add the pieces of boiled chicken, and boil for 10 minutes in the sauce.

Put a piece of chicken on each plate, cover it with the *mole* sauce, garnish with sesame seeds and serve immediately.

Chiles Rellenos de Queso o Picadillo

(chiles poblanos stuffed with cheese or meat)

12 *chiles* poblanos
1/2 *cup ground veal*
1/2 *cup ground pork (with 30 percent fat content)*
Salt and pepper to taste
1/4 *cup oil*
1 *medium onion, finely chopped*
1/8 *cup almonds, peeled and chopped*
1/8 *cup pine nuts*
1/8 *cup* acitrón
1/8 *cup raisins*
14 *ounces* morral *cheese* *
1/4 *cup oil*
1 *medium onion, finely chopped*
4 *cloves garlic*
8 *tomatoes, peeled, seeded and ground*
2 *cups chicken or beef stock (see index)*
2 *bay leaves*
1/4 *teaspoon powdered thyme*
Salt to taste
3 *sprigs fresh parsley, finely chopped*
1/4 *cup flour*
6 *egg whites*
6 *egg yolks*
1 1/2 *cups oil*

* *Jack or Muenster cheese may also be used.*

Toast the chiles over an open flame or under a broiler until they blister and char slightly. Wrap them in a cloth for 30 minutes to allow them to "sweat," then remove the skin. Open the chiles lengthwise, taking care that the stems do not become detached. Remove the seeds and veins, then wash and drain the chiles.

Combine the ground meats in a mixing bowl, and season with salt and pepper.

Fry the onion lightly in 1/4 cup of hot oil. Add the meat and mix well. Add the chopped almonds, pine nuts, *acitrón* and raisins. Continue cooking, stirring constantly, until the meat is cooked. Stuff six chiles with the meat mixture.

Cut the cheese into thick strips, and put two strips inside each remaining chile.

Heat 1/4 cup of oil in a skillet, and fry the onion and garlic lightly. Add the tomatoes and stir until the mixture forms a smooth paste. Add the broth, bay leaves and thyme. Add salt to taste, and cook for 10 minutes, then remove from the stove, strain, add the parsley and keep warm.

Use toothpicks to hold the chiles together. Roll them in flour until they are lightly coated. Beat the egg whites until stiff, then fold in the beaten egg yolks. Dip the chiles one by one into the egg mixture, and then fry them in 1 1/2 cups of hot oil until they are golden brown. Drain on absorbent paper.

Place the chiles gently into the tomato sauce. Serve on hot plates, covered with the sauce.

Chiles en Nogada

(stuffed chiles with walnut sauce)

12 *chiles* poblanos
1 cup ground veal
1 cup ground pork (with 30 percent fat content)
Salt and pepper to taste
1/4 cup cooking oil
1/2 medium onion, finely chopped
1/2 cup almonds, peeled and chopped
1/2 cup pine nuts
1/2 cup acitrón
1/2 cup raisins
1 1/2 cups fresh walnuts, skinned
1 cup milk
1 cup cream
Seeds from two ripe pomegranates
1 tablespoon fresh parsley, finely chopped

Toast the chiles over an open flame or under a broiler until they blister and char slightly. Wrap them in a cloth for 30 minutes to allow them to "sweat," then remove the skins and make a vertical slit down the sides. Remove the veins and seeds, taking care that the stems do not become detached. Drain.

Mix the veal and pork in a separate bowl. Season with salt and pepper.

Heat the oil and fry the onion lightly. Add the ground meat and mix well. Add the almonds, pine nuts, *acitrón* and raisins. Stir constantly until the meat is cooked. Remove the mixture from the fire and let cool. Stuff the chiles with the meat mixture, fasten them shut with toothpicks and put them on a platter.

Grind the walnuts. Add the milk slowly, stirring constantly, until the mixture is thick. Then add the cream and mix well. Cover the chiles with the cold walnut sauce.

Garnish the chiles with pomegranate seeds and parsley.

Note: This dish is usually served in August, when walnuts and pomegranates are in season in Mexico.

Pollo en Salsa de Almendra

(chicken in almond sauce)

1 1/2 chickens, cut in quarters
4 cups chicken stock (see index)
1/8 cup oil
3 ounces almonds, with skins
1 onion, chopped
3 cloves garlic
2 whole cloves
1/2 hard roll, sliced in rounds
1 small cinnamon stick
3 tomatoes, peeled, seeded and chopped
2 tablespoons oil
3 cups chicken stock
1 cup sherry or white wine
Salt to taste
1 teaspoon pepper
25 whole green olives
6 chiles largos, *canned*

Cook the chicken in the stock until it is tender. Remove the skin.

Fry the almonds in 1/8 cup of oil, and drain, saving the oil.

Then fry the onion, garlic, cloves, bread and cinnamon in this oil. Add the chopped tomatoes. When the mixture is well cooked, grind it together with the almonds to form a smooth paste. Chicken stock can be added if necessary.

Brown the chicken in 2 tablespoons of oil. Add the almond mixture, the stock and the sherry. Season with salt and pepper and simmer over low heat for approximately 30 minutes.

Add the olives and chiles. Correct the seasoning, and let simmer for five more minutes. Serve on hot ceramic or earthenware plates.

Pollo Manchamanteles

(chicken stewed with fruits and vegetables)

1 large chicken
5 chiles anchos
1 cup chicken stock (see index)
1/4 cup oil, or 2 tablespoons lard
1/2 medium onion, chopped
2 cloves garlic
2 whole cloves
1 tablespoon peanuts, shelled and peeled
1 slice white bread, with crust removed
1 small cinnamon stick
2 tablespoons oil
3 cups chicken stock
1 tablespoon vinegar
1 tablespoon sugar
2 tomatoes, peeled, seeded and ground
2 green apples, peeled and cut into large chunks
1 plantain, cut into thick slices
1/2 pound dried prunes
2 slices fresh pineapple, cut into large cubes
1 large sweet potato, baked, peeled and cut into large chunks

Cut the chicken into serving pieces, and cook in stock until tender.

Soak the chiles in chicken stock until they are soft. Remove from the stock, and remove the veins, seeds and stems. Drain.

Fry the onion, garlic, cloves, peanuts, bread and cinnamon in the hot oil or lard. When they are browned, remove them from the oil, drain well, and grind with the chiles. Return them to the frying pan with 2 tablespoons of oil and add the stock, vinegar, sugar and tomatoes. Cook until the liquid boils. Skim off the fat.

Add the chicken, and cook until the mixture comes to a boil again. Add the fruits one by one at five-minute intervals in the following sequence: (1) apples, (2) plantain, (3) prunes, (4) pineapple, and (5) sweet potato. Put the chicken and the fruit in the bottom of a warm deep serving dish, and pour the sauce over them. Serve immediately.

Pato en Pipián Verde

(duck in green pumpkinseed sauce)

2 ducks
8 leaves romaine lettuce
8 green tomatoes
2 cloves garlic
1 medium onion
10 sprigs fresh coriander
2 sprigs epazote
2 avocado leaves
1 teaspoon powdered cumin
2 chiles serranos
1/2 cup water
1 cup duck fat
2 cups pumpkinseeds, ground
3 cups chicken stock (see index)

Roast the ducks in the oven at medium heat (about 350°). Remove when tender, and cool. Reserve one cup of duck fat.

Grind the lettuce, tomatoes, garlic, onion, coriander, *epcazote,* avocado leaves, cumin and chiles with the water until the mixture forms a smooth paste.

Heat the duck fat in a frying pan. When it is hot, add the mixture and stir with a wooden spoon until the ingredients are well cooked. Add the pumpkinseeds and continue stirring until the mixture blends into a smooth paste. Add the hot chicken stock, and stir until the liquid comes to a boil.

Cut the duck into serving portions. Put the portions into the sauce, and let them stand for 15 minutes.

Serve in a hot serving dish. Accompany with hot tortillas.

Cochinita Pibil

(barbecued pork, Yucatán style)

2 *ounces* achiote
1/2 *cup vinegar*
3 *chiles* anchos, *toasted, with the seeds and veins removed*
1/2 *cup water*
1/2 *onion*
2 *cloves garlic*
1 *tomato*
4 *whole allspice*
1/2 *teaspoon oregano*
Salt to taste
2 *pounds leg, loin or flank of pork*
4 Bermuda *onions, sliced into rings*
1 *cup vinegar*
4 *banana leaves*
Tortillas
Xnipec Sauce (see index)

Mix the *achiote* with the vinegar.

Soak the chiles for 15 minutes in water.

Toast the onion, garlic and tomato on a hot griddle. Grind the toasted vegetables together with the chiles, cloves, oregano, allspice and *achiote* until they form a smooth paste. Strain. Correct the seasoning.

Cut meat into large chunks. Cover with the paste and marinate for 4 hours.

Marinate the onion rings for 2 or 3 hours in vinegar.

Use the banana leaves to line the bottom of a large earthenware casserole or suitable roasting pan. Put the meat on top of the leaves, and cover it with more leaves wrapping tightly. Roast the meat for about 1 1/2 hours, basting it periodically with the sauce. If the meat becomes dry, add water to the sauce.

The meat will be ready when it softens and begins to disintegrate. The sauce should be thick.

Arrange the meat on a hot serving platter, pour the sauce over it and garnish with the marinated onion rings. Serve with hot tortillas and *Xnipec* sauce.

Mixiote de Carnero

(seasoned lamb, wrapped in maguey leaves and steamed)

2 *chiles* guajillos
10 *chiles* anchos
5 cloves garlic
4 *whole cloves*
5 *cumin seeds*
3 *peppercorns*
Salt to taste
2 pounds lamb
1 tablespoon vinegar
2 tablespoons lamb fat
6 *tender* maguey *leaves, washed and soaked in
    water**
String

Boil the chiles in water until they are tender.
Remove the veins, seeds and stems.

Grind the chiles, garlic, cloves, cumin, peppercorns and salt into a smooth paste.

Cut the lamb into small chunks, and toss in
vinegar. Cover the meat with the chile paste, and
let stand for two hours.

Spread lamb fat over each *maguey* leaf. Put a
portion of meat and chile on each leaf. Fold the
leaf into a little bundle. Tie and cook the bundles
in a stearner for about two hours, or until the
meat is soft and tender.

* *Aluminum foil can be used if maguey leaves are
unavailable.*

Carnitas de Cerdo a la Queretana

(pork, Querétaro style)

6 1/2 pounds pork (spareribs, skin, loin, shoulder, ears, etc.)
2 cups milk
Salt to taste
5 quarts melted pork fat or lard
1 head of garlic, cut in half horizontally
1 sprig fresh thyme
2 bay leaves
2 small sticks cinnamon
Tortillas
Guacamole (see index)

Cut the meat into large chunks about 6 to 8 inches in diameter. Soak the meat in milk. Add salt.

Heat the fat in a large, deep iron pot over a high heat. When the fat is very hot, add the meat. The fat should cover the meat completely. Bring the fat to a boil, then add garlic, thyme, bay leaves and cinnamon. When the meat begins to brown, lower the heat and continue to cook for 2 or 3 hours. Stir occasionally to keep the meat from sticking to the sides of the pot.

Fifteen minutes before serving, cook the meat over a high heat so that it gets dark brown and crisp on the outside.

Remove the meat from the fat. Drain well. Cut into smaller pieces and serve with hot tortillas, *guacamole* and a variety of sauces (see index "Sauces and Chiles").

Tapado de Lengua de Res

(beef tongue stew)

1 large beef tongue
1 large onion, quartered
Salt to taste
4 chiles poblanos
1/8 cup oil
2 medium onions, finely chopped
4 cloves garlic, finely chopped
2 tomatoes, peeled, seeded and finely chopped
2 whole cloves
1 bay leaf
20 peppercorns
Salt to taste
1/4 Cup oil
4 large potatoes parboiled, peeled and cut into large chunks
30 almonds, peeled and chopped
30 green olives
2 cups orange juice

Place the tongue in a pot with the onion and salt, and cover with water. Simmer until cooked (about 3 hours). Remove the tongue from the pot. Remove the skin, and cut into horizontal slices.

Roast the chiles over an open flame or under a broiler until they blister and char slightly. Wrap them in a cloth or plastic bag for 30 minutes to "sweat." Remove the skin and veins, and mince.

Heat 1/8 cup of oil in a deep frying pan. Lightly fry the chopped onion, garlic and chiles, and add the chopped tomatoes. Continue cooking, stirring constantly until all ingredients have been blended evenly.

Combine the spices, grind, and add them to the tomato sauce.

Oil the bottom and sides of an oven-proof dish. Fill with alternating layers of sauce and meat. Arrange the potatoes, almonds and olives evenly over the top. Then sprinkle orange juice over.

Cook in a slow oven (about 300°) until the potatoes are done.

Take out the pieces of tongue and arrange in the form of a fan on a warm serving dish. Cover with the sauce, and place the potatoes and olives alongside.

Tamales Rojos, Verdes y Dulces

(red, green and sweet tamales)

2 pounds lard
3 cups beef or chicken stock, depending on the
    meat used (see index)
2.2 pounds of tamal flour
1 cup water, in which the husks of Mexican green
tomatoes have been boiled
1 teaspoon baking powder
1 teaspoon salt
2.2 pounds cooked pork or chicken
2 cups mole poblano (see index)
2 cups green sauce (see index)
2 cups sugar
2 teaspoons aniseed
1/4 cup raisins
1/4 cup acitrón, chopped
30 dried corn cob leaves

Beat the lard with 1 cup of the stock, until it is fluffy and smooth. Test by dropping a bit of the mixture into water. If it floats, it has been sufficiently beaten; if it sinks, continue beating. Add the flour slowly, alternating with the broth and the tomato water. Add baking powder and salt. The dough should be compact, but not hard.

Separate the dough into three parts.

Finely chop meat into small pieces. Separate into two parts.

For red tamales, heat the *mole*.

For green tamales, heat the green sauce.

For sweet tamales, incorporate the sugar, aniseed, raisins and *acitrón* into one part of the dough.

Soak the corn leaves in hot water, until they are soft and pliable.

For red and green tamales:
Open the leaf. Spread a thin coating of dough over an area about 3 x 3 inches in the center of the leaf (use about a tablespoon of dough). Put 1 tablespoon of meat, then 1 of sauce, on top of the dough. Fold the long sides of the leaf over the dough, then fold the tips over the center, and tie shut with string or a thin strip of leaf.

For sweet tamales:
Spread a thin coating of the dough to which sugar and other ingredients were added, on an area about 3 x 3 inches. Close the tamales as above.

Place the tamales upright in the top of a steamer, and cook until the dough separates easily from the leaf (about 2 1/2 to 3 hours). Serve hot.

Note: Bean tamales can be made by substituting refried beans (see index) for the meat and sauce.

Tamales Rojos

Tamales Dulces

Salpicón

(shredded meat)

2 quarts water
1 medium onion, quartered
2 bay leaves
1/2 teaspoon powdered thyme
1 leek
2 stalks celery
Salt and pepper to taste
3 1/2 pounds flank steak
4 large cooked potatoes, cubed
8 tablespoons olive oil
6 tablespoons vinegar
1 medium onion, sliced and blanched
1/2 head of lettuce, finely chopped
Salt and black pepper to taste
3 avocados, cut into long strips
6 radishes, sliced
2 tomatoes, sliced

Heat the water in a deep pan. Add quartered onion, bay leaves, thyme, leek and celery. Season with salt and pepper. When the water comes to a boil, add the meat and continue cooking. The meat will be done when a small piece can be pulled off easily and the meat below is pink. When it is done, remove it from the water, let cool and shred.

Add the potatoes, olive oil, vinegar, sliced onion and lettuce to the shredded meat. Season with salt and pepper, and mix thoroughly. Arrange the meat on a platter.

Garnish with avocados, radishes and tomatoes. Serve cold. Chiles *chipotles,* or pickled chiles *jalapeños* or *serranos* can be served on the side. *Salpicón* tastes even better when eaten with bread.

Albóndigas en Chipotle
(meatballs in chile chipotle sauce)

1 pound ground beef
1 pound ground pork (with 30 percent fat content)
Salt and pepper to taste
1 cup cooked rice
3 egg yolks
1 slice bread, soaked in milk
3 fresh mint leaves, finely chopped
2 hard-boiled eggs, diced
1/8 cup oil
1 medium onion, ground
2 cloves of garlic, ground
8 tomatoes, roasted and ground
1 pinch of powdered cumin
2 chiles chipotles adobados *(canned), ground*
2 cups beef stock, (see index)
Salt to taste
3 fresh mint leaves, finely chopped
Tortillas

Mix the beef and pork together. Season with salt and pepper. Add cooked rice, egg yolks, bread and mint, and mix well. Make 1 inch meatballs, each with a piece of hard-boiled egg in the center. Let stand.

Heat the oil in a deep frying pan. Fry onion and garlic lightly. Add the ground tomatoes, cumin and chiles, stirring constantly to form a paste. Add the stock, and stir constantly over a low heat until the sauce comes to a boil. Add the salt and the mint. Put the meatballs into the sauce one by one, taking care that they don't disintegrate. Simmer about 1 hour, until the meat is cooked.

Serve with hot tortillas.

Pozole de Jalisco

(corn soup, Jalisco style)

*5 cups whole hominy kernels, or large, white,
dried corn kernels*
1/2 cup unslaked lime
8 cups water
1 1/4 pounds boneless pork, cut into chunks
2 pigs' feet, cleaned and cut into chunks
6 cups water
1 onion, quartered
1/2 head garlic
2 bay leaves
1 sprig fresh thyme
Salt to taste
1/2 head lettuce, finely chopped
1 onion, chopped
3 radishes, chopped
6 tablespoons powdered oregano
10 chiles piquín, finely powdered
Optional: lime wedges

Boil the corn in lime and water until it puffs up
and its skin loosens. Remove the corn, and let
cool. Rinse it, and remove the skins by rubbing the
kernels together briskly. Remove the kernel tips.
Set clean kernels aside in a bowl of water.

Clean the meat and cook it with water, onion,
garlic, bay leaves, thyme and salt, over a medium
heat, until the meat is tender. Add more water if
necessary. Remove the meat and strain the broth.
Reheat the broth, adding meat and corn. Cook
until the corn pops open or "flowers."

Serve the soup in hot bowls. Serve the lettuce,
onion, radishes, powdered oregano and chile, in
separate dishes, so that each person may garnish
his or her soup according to taste. Lime wedges
can also be included as a garnish.

Serve with *totopos*.

Rice & Beans

FRIJOLES: THE UBIQUITOUS BEANS

Frijoles is the Mexican word for beans, a national staple. *Frijoles* are often on the menu for breakfast, lunch and dinner. For the big meal of the day, eaten between two and five o'clock in the afternoon, they appear in the form of soup or as a complement to meats and stews, or as a dessert. For the poor, *frijoles* are a meal in themselves.

Frijoles play an important part in the way Mexicans extend their hospitality. When an invitation is issued, the guests are often told to bring along their friends. If more people come than had been expected, the host will, as the saying goes, "add more water to the beans." In spirit, this means that there will always be enough food to go around.

Most of the types of beans we know today–lima beans, kidney beans, string beans and shell beans–are members of the same family and originate in Mexico. Some of the most popular of the nearly one hundred types of beans grown in Mexico today are the black *veracruzanos,* the beige *bayos,* the mottled *flor de mayos,* the white *alubias* and the mustard-colored *canarios,* seen in the picture opposite.

Frijoles possess high nutritional value. They are rich in amino acids, and when eaten in combination with other grains yield a protein nearly as complete as that of animal origin. This makes them a source of vital sustenance for millions of the world's poor. Vitamin B, iron, carbohydrates, phosphorous, fats and traces of other nutrients are also contained in what has been misnamed the "modest bean."

There are many ways of preparing *frijoles,* but all begin with hours of boiling, for, as the Mexicans say, "not even mice will eat raw beans." The simplest recipe is *frijoles de olla,* "from the pot." The beans are washed, and then boiled for several hours (until soft) in an earthenware pot with onion, a piece of pork or lard and perhaps a few *epazote* leaves. *Frijoles de olla* are garnished with chopped onions or chile and eaten as a soup in the rich broth produced by their cooking. *Frijoles a la charra* is a variation *of frijoles de olla* and is very popular in northern Mexico.

Another classic recipe is *frijoles refritos,* literally "refried beans," which accompany innumerable dishes from breakfast eggs to *carne a la tampiqueña,* meat Tampico style. A variation of this recipe comes from the Yucatán: Before the beans are fried, they are mashed and passed through a sieve to make a finely pureed paste for use in *panuchos, garnachas* and *huevos motuleños.*

Arroz a la Mexicana

(rice, Mexican style)

2 cups rice
1 cup oil
1/2 medium onion
2 chiles serranos
2 cloves garlic
2 sprigs parsley
3 tomatoes, skinned, seeded and ground
1 cup fresh peas
2 carrots, peeled, and diced
4 cups chicken stock (see index)
Salt to taste
2 tablespoons chopped parsley
2 hard-boiled eggs, sliced into rounds

Rinse the rice, drain it, and spread over a flat surface to dry.

Heat the oil in a frying pan and lightly fry the onion, chiles and garlic. Add the rice and fry until it turns a light brown. Add the parsley and tomatoes, stirring constantly. Add the peas, carrots and chicken stock. Add salt. Cover, and let simmer over a low heat for about 40 minutes. Remove the onion, chile, garlic and parsley.

Sprinkle chopped parsley over the rice and garnish with hard-boiled egg.

This rice is usually eaten with tortillas and a chile sauce (see index).

Arroz a la Poblana

(rice Puebla style)

2 *cups rice*
4 *chiles* poblanos
1 *cup oil*
1/2 *medium onion*
2 *cloves garlic*
1 *cup fresh corn kernels*
4 *cups chicken stock (page 22)*
1 *sprig fresh* epazote
Salt to taste
1/4 *cup cream*
Tortillas

Rinse the rice, drain it, spread it on a cookie sheet, and let stand in a warm place until dry.

Toast the chiles over an open flame or on a griddle until they char and blister slightly, then wrap them in a cloth and let them "sweat" for 30 minutes.

Remove the skins, veins, seeds and stems. Grind two chiles with about l/3 cup of the stock, and cut the other two into strips.

Heat the oil in a skillet. Fry the onion and garlic lightly. Add the rice and fry it until it turns a light brown. Add the ground chiles, stirring constantly. Add the corn kernels, chicken stock, *epazote* and chile strips. Season with salt. Cover, and let simmer over a low heat for about 40 minutes. Remove the onion, garlic and *epazote* before serving.

Pour cream over the rice, let stand for a few minutes, covered, then serve with hot tortillas.

Frijoles Refritos

(refried beans)

2 pounds beans (black, turtle, pink or pinto)
Water to cover
12 cups water
1 onion, halved
3 sprigs fresh epazote
2 tablespoons pork fat or cooking oil
2 slices of onion

Clean beans, removing all stones or chaff. Rinse well, and let soak in water for two hours, then drain.

Add water to cover, and boil with the onion, *epazote* and salt until tender. Add water when necessary. Correct the seasoning. (At this stage, the beans have become frijoles *de olla* or "beans from the pot.")

Beans should not be kept in the refrigerator. Cover them and store in an open place, in the same pot in which they were cooked.

The next day, boil the beans again for a short time. Heat pork fat or oil in a frying pan. Fry the onion lightly, and add the beans, stirring constantly until they come to a boil. Traditionally, this process is repeated daily until all the beans have been eaten.

Frijoles Maneados

(puree of beans with cheese and chile *ancho)*

3/4 *cup oil*
3 *chiles* serranos, *cut into thin rounds*
3 *cups refried beans (see index)*
1 *cup* asadero *cheese, cubed**
12 totopos

Heat the oil in a frying pan, and fry the chiles lightly. Add the refried beans. Mash with a wooden spoon until they form a paste. Add the cheese, stirring constantly. Correct the seasoning, garnish with *totopos,* and serve immediately.

*Any good melting cheese may be substituted.

53

Sauces & Chiles

CHILES: THE SPICE OF MEXICAN LIFE

If corn is the *modus vivendi,* and tortillas the *modus operandi,* then chiles are the *chiste,* the punch, fun and flavor of the Mexican diet. A tasty chile sauce is usually enough to rescue a meal of tortillas and beans from blandness.

Since Columbus believed he had discovered the Spice Islands, he assumed that the exotic and piquant fruit he ate in Santo Domingo was a theretofore unknown variety of pepper. He wrote to his patron, King Ferdinand of Spain, that he had found "pepper in a pod, with a flavor that is very strong but is not the same as that of the pepper of the East." But Columbus had discovered neither the Spice Islands nor pepper, but America and chile.

Shortly after the Conquest, chile plants were taken to the Old World and integrated in varying degrees into the cuisines of many European countries. In Spain, for example, the sweet red pimiento was cultivated and used to adorn *paella,* and in the Orient, the hottest chiles were used to enliven and fire up traditional dishes.

In the middle of the nineteenth century, an American soldier who had fought in the Mexican War returned to his native Louisiana with some seeds of a particularly fiery variety of chile he had found in the state of Tabasco. When the plants were cultivated and their fruit was fermented in oak barrels with salt and vinegar, the produce became the well-known Tabasco sauce, the burning drops of which enliven everything they touch, from a Bloody Mary to a plate of fresh oysters.

Chile, a bushy, woody-stemmed shrub, comes in many varieties, with fruits of many sizes–from long and conical to tiny, twisted and hard–and in many colors, from parrot green to ecclesiastical purple, and in many degrees of piquancy, from mild to incandescent. Some chiles are eaten fresh like the chile *serrano,* cooked or pickled like the chile *jalapeño,* while others are left to ripen and dry on the plant like the chile *ancho.* The veins and seeds of most chiles are so hot that one must have a tin-lined throat to swallow them–yet the degree hotness is difficult to predict. The intensity of flavors of different chiles from a single plant can vary from burning hot to bland, a phenomenon for which no acceptable botanical explanation has been found. However, a discriminating cook can handle such differences. Chiles have more than flavor. They contain substantial amounts of vitamins A and C, and since pre-Hispanic days, people have believed that, taken in moderation they help the digestive process.

It would be an awesome task to describe the chiles of Mexico, as over half of the two hundred known types in the world are grown there. A selection of some of the most common ones are shown in the photograph opposite. Although chiles provide some of the dominant flavors in Mexican cooking, Mexican cuisine is full of other surprising nuances and subtleties, many of which are included in the recipes of this book.

54

Chiles en Conserva

(pickled chiles)

Any kind of fresh chile can be pickled, but the only dried chile that can be so preserved is the *chipotle.*

Many vinegars–grape, wine, pineapple, sugar cane, apple, and so on–can be used, and each provides its own distinctive flavor. Three ingredients are essential: garlic, onion and carrots. Spices and herbs such as bay leaves, thyme, marjoram, rosemary, aniseed and sage among others, either individually or in varying combinations, may be added according to taste.

4 cups vinegar
1 pound chiles
2 carrots, cut into rounds
2 whole heads of garlic
1 medium onion, quartered
Herbs to taste
Salt to taste

Put the ingredients in a sterilized glass container. Cover and let stand about 2 weeks, to season. Keep the container in an open place, but away from direct sunlight.

55

Guacamole

(puree of avocado with onion and coriander)

6 large avocados
1 tablespoon olive oil
1/2 medium onion, finely chopped
3 chiles serranos, finely chopped
Salt to taste
2 sprigs fresh coriander, finely chopped

Mash the avocados with olive oil. Add the onion, chiles, salt and coriander, and mix thoroughly.
Serve in an earthenware dish or a *molcajete*.

Salsa Verde

(green tomato sauce)

12 Mexican green tomatoes, without husks
4 chiles serranos
1/2 medium onion, finely chopped
1 clove garlic
1 tablespoon chopped coriander
Salt to taste

Wash the tomatoes and chiles, and toast with the onion and garlic on a *comal* or hot griddle, until they blister and brown slightly. Grind all ingredients in a *molcajete* or stone mortar. Add the coriander and salt, and mix well.

Salsa Ranchera

(a cooked red tomato sauce)

2 large tomatoes
3 chiles serranos, without stems
1/2 onion, finely chopped
1 clove garlic
Salt to taste
1 tablespoon oil

Parboil the tomatoes and chiles. Peel the tomatoes.

Grind the tomatoes and chiles in a *molcajete* or stone mortar with the onion and garlic. When they are evenly ground, add salt.

Heat the oil in a frying pan, and fry the ground mixture until it is well cooked.

Serve in an earthenware dish.

Salsa Mexicana

(an uncooked sauce of tomato, onion and chile)

3 tomatoes, chopped
3/4 medium onion, finely chopped
2 sprigs fresh coriander, finely chopped
6 chiles serranos, *finely chopped*
Salt to taste

Mix all ingredients. If the mixture becomes too thick, add a bit of water.

Serve the sauce in a *molcajete* or earthenware dish.

Salsa Borracha

(sauce with chile pasilla, beer and orange juice)

6 chiles pasilla
1 cup pulque *or beer*
Juice of 1 orange
Salt to taste
l/2 clove garlic
1/4 onion, finely chopped
15 whole green olives
1/2 cup mild white cheese, crumbled

Toast the chiles on a *comal* or griddle until they char slightly and the skin blisters. Open them, remove the veins, seeds and stems, and soak for 20 minutes in the *pulque*.

Grind the chiles with the *pulque,* orange juice, salt and garlic.

Add the onion, olives and cheese, and mix thoroughly. Before serving, sprinkle some more of the crumbled cheese over the sauce.

Salsa Cascabel

(sauce of chile cascabel)

8 Mexican green tomatoes, without husks
5 chiles cascabel
3 cloves garlic
1/4 onion
Salt to taste

Toast the tomatoes, chiles, garlic and onion on a *comal* or hot griddle until they are lightly charred. Grind all ingredients together, and add salt to taste.

Serve in a *molcajete* or earthenware dish.

Salsa Xnipec

(a hot sauce from Yucatán)

1 small onion, finely chopped
1 chile habanero, *washed, with the veins and seeds*
extracted, and finely chopped
Juice of 2 Seville oranges *
Salt to taste

Soak the onion and chile for one hour in juice.
Add salt.

    This sauce is served with *Cochinita Pibil* (see
index).

* *The juice of another citrus fruit. or a light, fruity*
vinegar, may be substituted.

Desserts

CHOCOLATE: A GIFT FROM THE GODS
Chocolate lovers the world over know, deep in
their hearts, that chocolate must have come from
heaven. Few, however, realize that it was a Toltec
heaven.

According to legend, to relieve the people from
their toil and suffering, the gods selected
Quetzalcoatl, the god of light, to assume human
form and rule the Toltecs. His reign brought great
happiness and prosperity. Before returning to
heaven, Quetzalcoatl stole *cacao* from the gods
and gave it to his beloved people on earth. He
taught them how to cultivate it and how to prepare the heavenly drink from it.

Myth aside, *cacao* was first cultivated in pre-
Hispanic Mexico and a cold, foamy drink prepared from it. Various herbs and spices were
mixed in, and there was white, orange and black
chocolate. The word *chocolate* comes from the
Nahuatl, the language of the Aztecs, although the
exact etymology is uncertain. Chocolate, under-
standably, quickly became a favorite food of the
conquistadors. Cortés wrote to his king that
chocolate "improved the natural defenses of one's
organism, and defended against fatigue."

Chocolate was rapidly incorporated into the
Spanish diet and spread to other European countries. A Spanish attendant to Queen Maria
Theresa, wife of Louis XIV, introduced chocolate
to the court of Versailles. Alexander von
Humboldt, the scientist and traveler, is credited
with popularizing chocolate in Germany, and
making an addict of the poet-philosopher Johann
Wolfgang von Goethe.

Curiously, the English at first seem impervious
to the blandishments of chocolate. English pirates
referred to chocolate as "sheep's dung" and once
threw a cargo of it overboard from a captured
Spanish ship. In the middle of the seventeenth
century though, the English had succumbed and
chocolate was selling at premium prices in London
shops. In Mexico today, hot chocolate is prepared
in much the same way as it was in pre-Hispanic
times. A wooden stirrer called a *molinillo* is spun
around in the drink to create the proper frothi-
ness.

Pastel de Elote

(corn cake)

10 ounces butter
1 1/2 cups flour
1 egg
1 cup sugar
1 cup milk
2 tablespoons cornstarch
3 egg yolks
1 teaspoon vanilla
1/4 cup sugar
7 ounces butter
3/4 cup sugar
3 eggs
1 cup sifted flour
Ground kernels of 3 fresh ears of corn

Soften the butter. Spread the flour over a flat, wooden or stainless-steel working surface, and make a hollow in the middle. Put the butter, egg and sugar in the hollow. Mix the ingredients by hand, incorporating the flour little by little. Knead the ingredients until they become a smooth dough. Use a floured rolling pin to roll the dough to form a flat 1/4-inch-thick disc and press the dough into a greased pie tin, molding it to the sides and bottom.

Dissolve the cornstarch in a tablespoon of the milk. Add the egg yolks and vanilla. Heat the rest of the milk, and when it comes to a boil, add 1/4 cup of sugar. Lower the heat, and add the cornstarch mixture, stirring constantly until it thickens.

Beat the butter until it is soft, and then gradually add 3/4 cup of sugar. Beat again until the butter and sugar become light and fluffy. Add the eggs, one by one, beating constantly. Add the thickened eggs and vanilla, the flour and corn. Mix thoroughly.

Pour the mixture into the pie tin and bake in a 350° oven for about 40 minutes, or until it is set. Cool and serve.

Jericalla

(custard)

3 cups milk
1 cup sugar
1 small cinnamon stick
2 eggs
3 egg yolks
1 tablespoon butter

Bring milk, sugar and cinnamon to a boil, then let cool.

Beat eggs together with egg yolks. Add one cup of the milk mixture. Mix thoroughly, then add the remaining milk. Strain.

Grease a baking dish with butter, and fill it with the mixture. Place dish in a pan of water, and bake in a moderate oven (about 350°) until the custard sets and the top is golden brown. Cool and serve.

Note: This custard can also be prepared in individual Pyrex dishes.

Calabaza en Tacha

(sweetened pumpkin)

1 large pumpkin
2 cups water
1 1/2 pounds dark brown sugar (or 3 cones of piloncillo) *cut into small pieces*
4 cinnamon sticks

Wash and clean out the pumpkin and cut it into chunks about 4 x 4 inches. Put the chunks in a saucepan with water. Sprinkle the brown sugar and cinnamon over the pumpkin. Simmer over low heat until the pumnkin is soft and the liquid is the consistency of honey.

Serve hot or cold.

Note: This dish can be served for breakfast, or as a dessert with hot or cold milk.

66

Postre de Piña y Almendras

(pineapple and almond dessert)

1 large pineapple
1 pound sugar
1/2 pound almonds, peeled and ground
1 egg white
6 egg yolks, beaten
1/2 pound almonds, halved

Peel the pineapple and grind it in a pan with a thick bottom. Cook the pineapple with the sugar over medium heat, stirring constantly with a wooden spoon until the mixture becomes very thick and shrinks from the sides of the pan.

Mix the ground almonds with egg white, and add them to the pineapple.

Heat the mixture until it thickens again and shrinks from the sides of the pan. Remove from heat, add egg yolks, and cook for five minutes more.

Serve the pineapple mixture garnished with the halved almonds.

Cocada

(coconut pudding)

5 cups finely grated fresh coconut
4 cups milk
3 cups sugar
4 egg yolks, beaten
2 heaping tablespoons chopped almonds

Put the coconut, milk and sugar in a pan with a thick bottom. Cook over a low heat, stirring constantly, until the mixture is blended. Remove from the heat and let stand for 15 minutes. Add the egg yolks slowly, beating constantly. When the ingredients are well mixed, return to the heat and cook until thick.

Put the mixture into a ovenproof dish, garnish with chopped almonds, and broil until the top is golden brown.

Chongos Zamoranos

(a clabbered milk dessert cooked in a cinnamon syrup)

8 cups milk
4 egg yolks
1/2 rennet tablet, or 5 drops of rennet
2 tablespoons water
2 cups sugar
3 small cinnamon sticks

Mix the milk and egg yolks in a copper or other heavy metal pan. Cook briefly over low heat until the mixture is lukewarm.

Dissolve the rennet in two tablespoons of water, add it to the mixture, and let stand in a warm place until it sets (about 1 hour).

Use a thin, sharp knife to cut the pudding into even 1- to 2-inch squares, cutting straight down to the bottom of the pan. Carefully fill the cracks between the squares with sugar, but do not allow sugar to fall on the surface of the squares. Put a little piece of cinnamon on top of each square. Cook over a very low heat for about 4 hours, or until the liquid formed by the melted sugar is the consistency of honey. Remove from the fire and allow to cool.

Serve the dessert covered with the liquid.

Capirotada

(Mexican bread pudding)

4 hard rolls
1 1/2 cups oil
1 pound dark brown sugar (or 1 pound piloncillo*)*
6 cups water
2 sticks cinnamon
1/2 cup añejo *or cheddar cheese, crumbled*

Cut the rolls into thin slices, and fry in oil.

Cook the brown sugar, water and cinnamon over a medium heat. Boil until the sugar dissolves and the liquid is the consistency of honey.

Cover the bottom of a shallow dish with the bread slices. Pour the dissolved sugar over the top, sprinkle with cheese and let cool before serving.

Dulce de Nuez

(pecan dessert)

3 cups pecans
2 cups milk
4 egg yolks
l/2 cup sugar
2 tablespoons chopped pecans

Grind the pecans and milk to form a paste. Add egg yolks. Put mixture into a pan with a thick bottom. Cook it over a low heat, stirring constantly until thick. Add sugar and continue cooking, stirring constantly until the sugar has been thoroughly incorporated.

Put mixture in a serving dish and let cool. Sprinkle chopped pecans over top.

Dulce de Piñón

(pine nut dessert)

2 cups milk
3 cups pine nuts
2 egg yolks
1/2 cup sugar
1 tablespoon whole pine nuts

Grind pine nuts and milk to form a puree. Add egg yolks, stir, and cook over a low heat in a heavy metal or copper pan. When the mixture thickens, add sugar and stir until blended.

Place the mixture on a serving platter and let cool. Garnish with whole pine nuts.

Arroz con Leche

(rice pudding)

2 cups rice
6 cups milk
2 1/2 cups sugar
4 small cinnamon sticks

Rinse the rice. Soak in water to cover. Drain, spread over a flat surface and allow to dry.

Combine the rice and milk in a pan with a thick bottom. Cook over a low heat, but do not boil. When the rice is soft, add the sugar and cinnamon, and continue cooking, stirring constantly until the ingredients thicken and the rice is cooked.

Cool, sprinkle cinnamon over the surface and serve in a deep dish.

Note: This dessert can be served with Mexican sweet rolls.

Drinks

THE MAGUEY: TREE OF MARVELS

The story of Mexican beverages would be incomplete without mention of the magnificent *maguey*, or century plant. This cactus provides the refreshing *aguamiel*, literally "honey water", which, when fermented, becomes *pulque*, and when distilled, becomes *tequila*. The *maguey* was so important to the Aztecs that it was deified in the form of the goddess Mayahuel, a fecund figure with 450 breasts from which she suckled the same number of children, the most important of whom was Ometecuhtli, the god of *pulque*.

The *maguey*, with its sharply pointed leaves like a huge spiky crown, dominates the landscape of central Mexico. It is a hardy succulent, withstanding extreme climatic conditions and thriving in the rockiest soil. It requires little care from planting to maturity. Almost every part of the *maguey* plant is used. *Aguamiel* that is not fermented to make *pulque* can be converted into honey, crystallized into a sugarlike substance or made into yeast or vinegar. The dried leaves provide a rough fiber from which rope can be made and when more finely worked, it is used as a sewing thread. The pulp from the mashed leaves is the raw material from which a parchmentlike paper is produced. The sharp spines are used as nails or sewing needles, and the dried plant is excellent fuel or good material for roofing. In cooking, the tender inner leaves become wrapping for *mixiotes* and the outer leaves are used to line barbecue pits. The flowers and the center stalks are eaten. The fleshy part of the leaves is mashed and mixed with corn *masa* to be patted into *maguey* tortillas. And–most delicious of all–the fat worms that thrive inside the leaves, when fried and eaten in tacos, are a veritable delight for daring gourmets. No wonder that the *maguey* has been called the "tree of marvels."

A great variety of ingredients, ranging from melon and celery to strawberries and chile, are added to the simple, classic *pulque* to give it different flavors. Such beverages are called *curados*. *Pulque* has a reputation of being the drink of the poor and for most it is an acquired taste.

Tequila drinking is a ceremony with a ritual of its own. Traditionally, one holds a piece of lemon in the left hand, then puts a pinch of salt in the cavity formed between the thumb and forefinger, and holds the slender tequila shot glass with the right hand. Before taking a drink, one licks the salt from the left hand, and then sucks on the lemon. *Sangrita*, a red beverage made from Seville oranges, grenadine, chile and spices is often served as a chaser to tequila. It has a refreshing aftertaste. Tequila is often mixed with nonalcoholic beverages to produce a variety of cocktails, the best known being the margarita, reportedly named after the courtesans who frequented bars and *cantinas* around the end of the nineteen century.

Café de Olla

(coffee made in an earthenware pot)

6 cups water
1 small stick cinnamon
2 whole cloves
3 ounces dark brown sugar, or piloncillo
1 square chocolate
3 ounces ground coffee

Bring water to a boil in an earthenware pot, then add the cinnamon, cloves, sugar and chocolate. When the liquid comes to a boil again, skim off the foam. Lower the heat and make sure the liquid does not boil. Add the coffee, and let it steep.

Serve the coffee with a ladle, dipping into the surface so as not to stir up the grounds.

Atole Blanco

(a sweet drink made from corn)

1 cup corn flour
1/2 cup rice flour
2 tablespoons cornstarch
2 cups water cups
6 cups water

Mix dry ingredients thoroughly. Add 2 cups of water slowly, stirring constantly to avoid lumps. Strain.

Add the rest of the water to the mixture, and boil until thick.

Serve hot sprinkled with small chunks of *piloncillo* or dark brown sugar.
Variations:
a. Orange leaves can be added to the liquid after it cooks.
b. Half-milk and half-water can be used, instead of all water. A cinnamon stick can be added.
c. To make *Atole de grano,* or *alole* with corn kernels: Combine a cup of water, the kernels from two ears of corn and three ounces of brown sugar or *piloneillo.* Boil until the mixture is the consistency of honey. Add this mixture to the hot *atole.* Bring to a boil, and serve immediately.

Atole Champurrado

(chocolate *atole*)

7 cups atole *(see index)*
Piloncillo *or brown sugar to taste*
2 squares chocolate

Cook the *atole*, *piloncillo* and chocolate over a medium heat, stirring constantly until the chocolate melts.

Serve hot in earthenware mugs or coffee cups.

Note: Milk can be added, if desired.

Chocolate a la Mexicana

(Mexican hot chocolate)

3 squares sweetened chocolate
8 cups milk

Put the milk and chocolate into an earthenware pot and cook over a low heat until the chocolate has melted. Stir constantly so that it does not stick to the pan.

When the chocolate comes to a boil, lower the heat and beat vigorously with a wisk or hand beater until a thick foam rises to the top.

Serve hot in earthenware mugs.

Agua de Piña

(pineapple drink)

1 small pineapple, peeled, cored, and diced
8 cups water
Sugar to taste
Ice to taste

Grind the pineapple and sugar together with two cups of the water, until a smooth paste is formed. Add the rest of the water, stirring until ingredients are blended. Add ice, and keep in the refrigerator until ready to serve.

Stir again before serving.

Horchata de Melón

(a sweet drink made from cantaloupe seeds)

Seeds from 3 cantaloupes
1 small cinnamon stick
8 cups water
Sugar to taste
Ice

Spread the seeds on a tray and allow to dry in a warm place. When dry, grind seeds with 1 cup of the water, cinnamon and sugar. Strain. Add the remaining water. Add ice, and keep in the refrigerator until ready to serve.

Stir thoroughly before serving.

Tepache

(fermented pineapple drink)

Rind of 1 pineapple
1/2 pound piloncillo *or dark brown sugar*
3 whole cloves
8 cups water

Wash the pineapple rind and put it into a pot with the *piloncillo,* cloves and water. Cover with a thin cloth. Let stand for 3 or 4 days in a warm place, until it ferments. Strain through a fine sieve, and refrigerate.

Serve cold.

Note: Ice should not be added to *tepache.*

Rompope

(Mexican eggnog)

8 cups milk
1 pound sugar
8 egg yolks
1/2 cup milk
2 small cinnamon sticks
1 cup brandy

Boil the sugar and milk for 15 minutes, stirring constantly to avoid burning.

Combine the egg yolks and milk, and add them to the hot milk. Add cinnamon, and boil until the liquid is the consistency of a thick sauce. Remove from heat and add the brandy. Cool, and store in glass containers.

Agua de Melón

(refreshing cantaloupe drink)

1 cantaloupe, seeded and cubed
8 cups water
Sugar to taste
Ice to taste

Blend cantaloupe and sugar with 2 cups of the water. Add remaining water and stir. Add ice, and refrigerate until ready to serve.
Stir before serving.

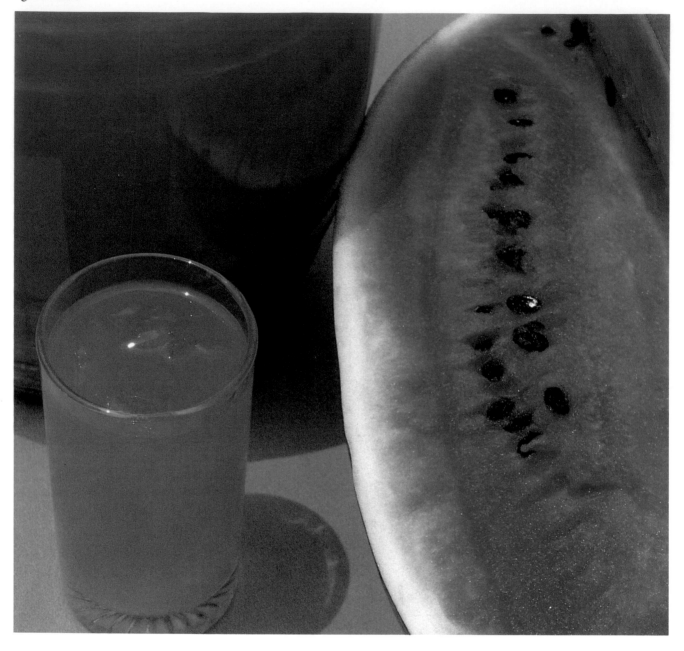

Agua de Sandía

(refreshing watermelon drink)

1 small watermelon, seeded and cubed
8 cups water
Sugar to taste
Ice to taste

Blend watermelon and sugar with 2 cups of the water. Add remaining and stir. Add ice, and refrigerate until ready to serve.
 Stir before serving.

Ponche de Frutas (Frío)

(cold fruit punch)

1 pound sugar
1 cup water
1 bottle white wine
1 bottle carbonated apple juice or cider
2 bottles carbonated mineral water
1 small watermelon chopped into bite-sized
chunks
2 cups strawberries, sliced

Mix the sugar and water. Cook until they form a syrup. Cool.

Add the wine, apple juice and mineral water to the syrup and mix thoroughly, then add the pieces of watermelon and the strawberries. Serve very cold.

Ponche de Frutas (Caliente)

(hot fruit punch)

1 scant cup of sugar
1 cup prunes
4 guavas, cut into pieces
3 oranges, peeled, seeded and cut into small pieces
10 crab apples
1 piece of sugar cane, cut into small pieces
1 cup brandy
10 cups water
2 cinnamon sticks

Put the sugar, fruit and cane into a deep pan. Cook until the sugar caramelizes and coats the fruit. Add the brandy and water. Cook until the fruit is soft. Serve hot.

Note: More brandy can be added, if desired.

Ponche Veracruzano

(fruit punch, Veracruz style)

3 ounces dried Jamaica flowers
8 cups water
15 crab apples
4 ten-inch sticks of sugar cane, peeled
2 cups sugar
2 small cinnamon sticks
Fruit to taste

Wash the Jamaica flowers in a strainer, and soak them in water for 24 hours, in a cool place. Strain, retaining water.

Add the crab apples and sugar cane to the flower water. Boil.

Heat the sugar in a hot skillet until it caramelizes, then add it to the hot punch. Strain. Add the cinnamon sticks and the finely chopped fruit.

Note: This punch can be served with or without rum.

Vocabulario

Words Commonly Used in Mexican Cooking

ACHIOTE
the hard seed of the annatto tree (*Bixa orellana*), ground to a powder to give flavor and a red color to certain foods, particularly dishes from Yucatán

ACITRÓN
see *Biznaga*

ADOBO
meat stewed in a thick sauce

AGUAMIEL
the sweet liquid from the *maguey,* or century plant

AGUARDIENTE
a liquor made from sugar cane

AJONJOLÍ
sesame seed

ALBÓNDIGA
meatball

ALMÍBAR
a sweet syrup

ANCHO (chile)
ripened, dried *chile poblano* (also called *chile pasilla* in some parts of Mexico)

ANTOJITO
literally, "little whim," an appetizer

ATE
a sweet paste made from the pulp of fruits cooked with sugar. *Ate* is also used as the final syllable after the name of a fruit, for example, *guavabate, membrillate,* etc.

BARBACOA
a pit in the ground in which meat covered with *maguey* leaves is placed for cooking. Lamb is the most popular meat in central Mexico for cooking this way

BIRRIA
a dish of highly seasoned meat, usually lamb or goat, typical of the state of Jalisco

BIZNAGA
a cushion-shaped cactus, crystallized with sugar to make a popular candy called *acitrón*

BOTANA
an appetizer usually served with drinks. Popular botanas are *chicharrón, tostadas, chalupas,* peanuts, etc.

BURRITOS or BURRITAS
tacos made with wheat-flour tortillas instead of corn tortillas. They are typical of the northern states of Mexico

CACAHUAZINTLE
hominy, a variety of corn with large, fleshy white kernels that is used to make *pozole*

CAJETA
a caramel-like sweet, traditionally made with a portion of goat's milk and sugar

CASCABEL (chile)
a small round chile

CAZUELA
an earthenware casserole

CEVICHE
a dish made basically of fish marinated in lime juice

CECINA
dried, salted meat, usually beef

CHALUPA
literally, "shallop or little rowboat," an oval-shaped thick tortilla garnished with a sauce and cheese or shredded meat, or both

CHAMPURRADO
a drink similar to *atole* made with water or milk, cornmeal and chocolate

CHAYOTE
vegetable pear

CHÍA
seeds from the *salvia hispánica*

CHICHARRÓN
crisp, fried pork skin

CHILACA (chile)
a long, thin dark-green chile

CHIPOTLE (chile)
a brown, smoked chile; a dried chile *jalapeño*

CHIQUIHUITE
a woven basket for tortillas

CHONGOS
a dessert made from cooked, sweetened milk curds

CHORIZO
a sausage made of ground pork and spices

CILANTRO
fresh coriander *(Coriandrum sativum)*

COMAL
originally, a round baking sheet of unglazed pottery; nowadays a thin metal griddle used for cooking tortillas

CUARESMEÑO (chile)
another name for chile *jalapeño*

CURADO
pulque with fruit flavors

ELOTE
corn on the cob

ENCHILADA
a tortilla dipped in a chile sauce and filled with a variety of ingredients, most commonly with cheese, meat or both

EPAZOTE
a strong, aromatic herb used in Mexican cooking, called "Mexican tea" or "wormseed" in English *(Chenopodium ambrosoides)*

ESCABECHE
a light pickle

ESTOFADO
a stew

FLAUTA
an extra-long, thin taco full of barbeque meat; a speciality of Jalisco

FRIJOLES
beans

GALLETA
a cracker or cookie

GARNACHA
a small disk of masa pinched up around the rim, covered with beans and sauces and eaten as an *antojito*

GORDA or GORDITA
a small, thick tortilla, usually covered with a sauce or chopped onion

GUACAMOLE
mashed avocado, onion, coriander and tomato

GUAJILLO (chile)
a long, narrow died chile used in many basic sauces in southeast Mexico

HABANERO (chile)
a small, smooth, light green chile, probably the hottest of all

HORCHATA
a refreshing, milky-looking drink, traditionally made from ground rice or ground dried melon seeds or almonds

HUACHINANGO
red snapper

HUITLACOCHE
a black fungus, sometimes referred to as "corn rot," that grows on the corn cob; it is one of the most highly prized Mexican delicacies

JALAPENO (chile)
a small, fat green chile named for Jalapa, the capital of the state of Veracruz

JÍCAMA
a white, sweetish, juicy bulb; it is sliced and eaten in salads or with lemon or chile, as an appetizer (*Pachyrrhizus erosus*).

LARGO (chile)
a long, thin, pale yellow-green chile

LIMA AGRIA
Citrus limetta, a bitter lime unique to Yucatecan cooking

LIMÓN
a small green Mexican lime, similar to the Key lime

MAGUEY
Agave americana, the century plant, from which *pulque* is made

MAÍZ
dried corn, maize

MASA
the dough made of corn kernels, boiled with unslaked lime, used for making tortillas

METATE
a flat, rectangular stone with three legs, used for grinding corn, chile, cacao, etc., by rolling a cylindrical stone pestle called a *metlalpil.*

MEZCAL
an intoxicating drink obtained from a variety of the *agave* plant

MIXIOTE
the membrane from the *maguey,* used to wrap seasoned meats for cooking

MOLCAJETE
a stone mortar used for grinding chile and sauces

MORONGA
blood sausage

MULATO (chile)
a large, triangular, dark brown chile

NAHUATL
the language spoken by the Toltecs, the Aztecs and other indigenous peoples of the central highlands.

NIXTAMAL
corn that has been boiled in lime water but has not yet been ground into the wet dough known as *masa*

NOPAL
the tender paddle-shaped leaves of the *nopal* cactus, eaten as a cooked vegetable

OLLA
a round earthenware pot

PAGUA
a variety of avocado that is large and has a hard green skin, but a less subtle flavor than the smaller, more highly prized one

PAN DULCE
sweet bread, or a sweet roll

PASILLA (chile)
dried chile *chilaca*

PEPITA
pumpkin seed

PIBIL
from the Mayan word *pib*, "where meat is barbecued," usually after wrapping in banana leaves

PICADILLO
a mixture of ground or shredded meat and other ingredients, used as a stuffing for *chiles rellenos*

PICANTE
hot, spicy

PILONCILLO
a cone of dark brown, unrefined sugar, with a strong molasses flavor

PINOLE
a sweetened and toasted corn flour sometimes eaten dry as dessert

PIPIÁN
a sauce made of ground pumpkin seeds, nuts, spices and chiles

PIQUÍN (chile)
a small red chile, very hot

POBLANO (chile)
a large, fleshy green chile, originally grown in the state of Puebla

POZOLE
a hearty soup made from the kernels of *cacahuazintle* corn and meat, and garnished with chopped lettuce, radishes, oregano and lime

PULQUE
a milky white fermented drink made from *aguamiel*, the liquid from the *maguey* cactus

QUESADILILA
a tortilla filled with cheese, *huitlacoche,* squash blossoms or some other filling, then folded over and fried

RAJA
a strip or thin slice, usually of chiles

ROBALO
a fish, snook or sea bass

ROMPOPE
Mexican eggnog, made of eggs, milk, cinnamon and sugar, and spiked with rum

ROMERO
rosemary (*Rosmarinus officinalis*)

SANGRÍA
a refreshing drink, like lemonade, to which red wine and chopped fruit have been added (of Spanish origin)

SANGRITA
a chaser for tequila and *mezcal*, usually made from Seville oranges, lime juice and chile; however, the ingredients of *sangrita* vary, sometimes including pepper and other spices

SERRANO (chile)
a small, smooth-skinned green chile, probably the most widely used

SOPA AGUADA
soups with a fair amount of liquid, literally, "watery soup"

SOPA SECA
cooked rice or pasta

SOPE
a small fried and garnished tortilla; a favorite *antojito*

TACO
a tortilla wrapped around a variety of fillings, sometimes fried in lard

TAMAL
corn dough, mixed with lard, wrapped in a folded leaf or corn husk and steamed

TEJOLOTE
stone pestle used for grinding food in the *molcajete*

TEQUILA
a liquor distilled from the cooked pineapplelike base of the *agave tequilana*. The name derives from the town of Tequila in the state of Jalisco, now the center for commercially made tequila

TOMATE VERDE
a small, tart, round green tomato with a papery husk, very popular for sauces

TOMILLO
thyme *(Thymus)*

TOSTADA
a tortilla that has been fried to a crisp, then garnished

TOTOPO
a pie-shaped piece of tortilla, fried to a crisp. *Totopos* are frequently used to adorn frijoles, and to scoop up *guacamole* or other food

TUNA
the prickly pear, the fruit of the mature *nopal* cactus

XTABENTUM
a distilled drink, made from the honey of a Mayan flower

Index

About the Author

Dolores Rojas, a lifetime resident of the Southwest, has always considered cooking among her favorite pastimes. Prior to her retirement she worked at numerous hotels and restaurants where she became an expert on authentic Mexican cooking.

Now a full-time freelance writer, *The Treasury of Mexican Cuisine* is her first book.